Workplace Savvy

Peace, Love, Health & Prosperity
Dianne Hoyd Sutton
January 2015

Workplace Savvy

A Guide to Gaining a Competitive Edge in Today's Workplace

Dianne Floyd Sutton

Author of *Workplace Etiquette: A Guide
to Surviving and Thriving in Today's Workplace*

With contributions from

Tim Stranges, The Timothy Group

Bernard Robinson, C.M.C., The Institute for Human Development

Bowerman Publishing
Frederick, Maryland

Chapter 5, Conflict Management, is based on the work of Tim Stranges of the Timothy Group, Conflict Resolution Services, who has given his permission for inclusion in this book. Tim is a certified mediator for the State of Maryland. For more information, contact tstranges@comcast.net.

Chapter 7 is the work of Bernard Robinson of the Institute for Human Development and is included in this book with his permission. Robinson is a Certified Management Consultant (CMC). For more information, contact him at thoughts@ihdinc.org.

Note to readers: This book contains information, suggestions, and opinions from the authors. It is intended to provide helpful and informative material on the subject matter covered. The use, misuse or interpretation of the materials, in whole or part, is the sole responsibility of the reader. If a reader requires personal assistance or advice, professional counseling and/or legal services should be consulted.

> For information about special discounts for bulk purchases for government, business, educational, or non-profit organizations, please contact seimpact@aol.com.

First Printing: December 2014

Contents

Chapter 6   Technology Etiquette   90

Chapter 7   Working in Groups   101

With Contributions by Bernard Robinson, C.M.C., Institute for Human Development

Chapter 10   Now You're the Boss!   208

Chapter 11   Making the Transition   228

Preface

What's New in *Workplace Savvy*

Why this book?

- *Because there are some skills that are still timely and relevant in today's workplace!*

- *Because what you don't know could hurt your career!*

- *Because individuals in the workplace need to continually grow!*

Workplace Savvy is not an extension of my first book, *Workplace Etiquette*, but a reference to the next level of professional development in the workplace. While there are overlaps of previous topics from the first book, the materials in this new book cover many additional topics and expand on previous topics. *Workplace Savvy* complements your formal development and training within the organization. New topics include personal branding, conflict management, cultural etiquette, and working in groups. New information has been added about physical appearance, political savvy, and communication skills. There is also a chapter on transitioning from employee to supervisor. Throughout the book are thoughts and quotes to inspire your thinking.

This book does not take the place of formal training within and outside of your organization. It serves as a supplement in moving your career forward and identifying what you may need to make it happen. This is not a textbook, but more a reference guide that gives insight into a variety of relevant workplace topics. More extensive treatment of some topics will have to wait for other books. Listed in the appendix are websites and books to further pursue the topics presented.

As always, comments are welcomed and can be sent to seimpact@aol.com.

Objectives of This Book

The objectives of this book are based on the definitions of the words *savvy* and *workplace*. *Savvy* defined: practical understanding, shrewdly informed, intelligence, common sense, astute. *Workplace* defined: the place where one is employed or customarily does work; lab, factory, home, office, warehouse.

1. Give practical understanding of creating success in group dynamic
2. Identify ways to become politically astute at any level
3. Create a personal career brand

How This Book Is Organized

This book is organized into chapters by specific topic. While the chapters can stand alone (you can read out of sequence and grasp the information) it is strongly suggested you work through chapter one on personal and work values to gain better understanding. Each chapter includes activities to reinforce the concepts presented.

For answers to your workplace etiquette questions, go to

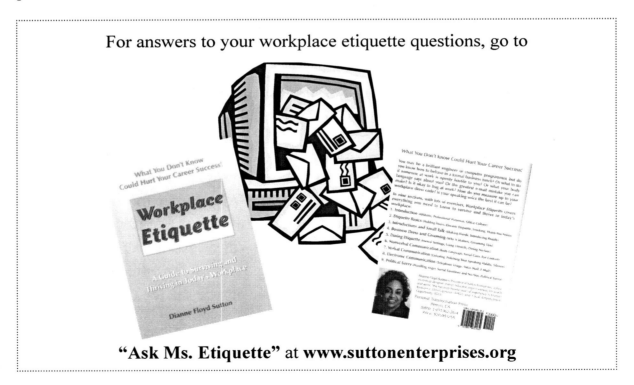

"Ask Ms. Etiquette" at **www.suttonenterprises.org**

Acknowledgments

A special acknowledgment to all my relatives in education: Willie Bright Woods (grandmother), Louise and David Finley (aunt and uncle), John T. Floyd (uncle), Phyllis Floyd Jones (aunt), Angela Finley Milton (cousin), and Rozsalind Brown (sister). I guess the education gene is in my DNA.

In truth, so many people have contributed extensively to my learning over the years that it is no longer possible to say precisely to whom I am indebted for which ideas in what form. However, HRD professionals Dick Dali, Robert Maddox, Bernard Robinson, Ben and Deb Alexander, Dr. JoAnn Peña, and Tim Stranges immediately come to mind.

A special shout-out to all the people who bought my first book, *Workplace Etiquette: A Guide to Surviving in Today's Workplace*, and who gave me feedback about the usefulness of its contents.

Many thanks to Tim Stranges and Rozsalind Brown for taking the time to carefully eye and give sharp critiques to my new material. Much love to my husband, Richard, for putting up with my long nights of frustration. I want to especially thank all those who read this book in various drafts and gave me the benefits of their feedback. Thank you SiRod Foster and Kristi Johnson Ford for your efforts.

Finally, I want to thank McKinley Gillespie, my friend and editor. No one contributed more to this book. From the very beginning she has organized every chapter and edited every word. I could not have done this without her expertise, enthusiasm, and energy.

First, a Quiz: What Do You Think?

This quiz is primarily a learning tool. For each statement below, circle A if you agree and D if you disagree. Your choices can vary depending on how you interpret the statements. Don't think about a score; just focus on the statements and application to your workplace. That is where the learning is contained.

1.	A D	Your cubicle is an extension of your professional presence.
2.	A D	Don't provide an agenda unless it is a large meeting.
3.	A D	Diversity encompasses much more than gender and race in the workplace.
4.	A D	Taking notes at a meeting is rude because you must break eye contact to do it.
5.	A D	Be careful about making critical comments about your organization, even if they are justified.
6.	A D	The "power perch" in meetings is the seat to the right of the head of the table.
7.	A D	If you want to appear important in meetings, sit as close to the leader as protocol permits.
8.	A D	People who are current on world events are generally considered current on business issues, too.
9.	A D	It is perfectly fine to paint your fingernails and eat in your cubicle and/or office.
10.	A D	Conflict is an unavoidable part of life.
11.	A D	The best way to handle a coworker who chit-chats is to look anxiously at your watch.
12.	A D	A wise strategy is to keep on good terms with everybody in your office even if you don't like everybody.
13.	A D	Cartoons and pictures lighten up e-mail messages to coworkers and are especially useful for sharing negative information.
14.	A D	Work-related social functions are usually a waste of personal time.
15.	A D	Your professional presence is comprised of all the resources you have to influence others.
16.	A D	Do not go out of your way to be nice to any employee in the organization who can't help you now or in the future.
17.	A D	If a customer is very pleased with the way you provided a service, ask the customer to write a complimentary note to your boss.

18.	A	D	All forms of office politics boil down to "butt kissing."
19.	A	D	It is better to be feared than respected by your subordinates.
20.	A	D	Don't be a complainer. It may be held against you.
21.	A	D	It's okay to tell ethnicity- and gender-related jokes in the office as long as members of the particular ethnic group or gender are not present.
22.	A	D	Business ethics apply only to people who work in the corporate world.
23.	A	D	As a supervisor, you can make all the decisions that affect your employees without getting their input.
24.	A	D	Conflict can be good.
25.	A	D	If someone in the office verbally abuses you or your coworkers, you should say something to them about the behavior.

The most workplace-savvy answers are listed on page 239.

Introduction

Why should your organization promote you?
For that matter, why did the organization hire you?
Who are you?
What do you have to offer?

These are the questions that I usually start off with in my seminars on workplace etiquette. You got hired; you are doing a good job; but you feel you are not progressing.

A lot of people believe that if they just do a good job, they will succeed—but that is not necessarily so. What happens when *everyone* is doing a good job? How do you distinguish yourself from the other members of the clan? How do you develop a competitive edge? Who are you?

Once you have established yourself in your position, there are three essential elements that constitute a formula for success at work: (1) performance, (2) image, and (3) exposure. Most people believe performance counts the most. However, once you have established yourself, image and exposure become much more important.

The Three Elements of Success

$$a^2 + b^2 = c^2$$

1. Performance

Includes: Your knowledge, skills, and abilities

Delivering results

Improving continuously

Practicing accountability

Listening

Being flexible

2. Image

Includes: Emotional intelligence (How you handle yourself and how you handle relationships)

Professional presence (The way you walk, talk, and dress)

Keeping commitments

Demonstrating integrity

Using tact and diplomacy

Being positive

3. Exposure

Includes: Networking

Meeting and greeting people within the organization

Volunteering for extra duties and activities

Using self-disclosure

Mental Notes and Action Items

1.   What does each of these concepts mean to you?
2.   How can you improve in each of these areas?

Performance:

Image:

Exposure:

> ### *The East Coast Hollywood*
> **D.C. Area Ranks as the Nation's Best-Educated**
>
> The Washington, D.C. area is the nation's best-educated metropolitan area, both in terms of bachelor's and graduate degrees. The region also boasts six of the nation's 10 best-educated counties, including the top five. So, if you are headed to D.C., be prepared to compete with all the superstars.

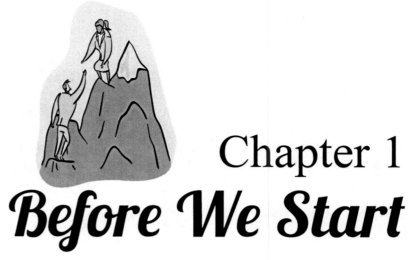

Chapter 1
Before We Start

Identifying Your Values

What's important to you?

Values are ideals, concepts, or beliefs that are important to you and influence your decisions. You have a core set of personal values whether you are consciously aware of it or not; often you do not realize what they are until you are forced into a difficult situation and must defend them to yourself or others. Values can range from the commonplace, such as the belief in hard work and punctuality, to the more psychological, such as self-reliance, concern for others, and harmony of purpose. If your life and career choices support your values, you will find greater satisfaction in both.

Give yourself focus in reading and using the information in this book—assess your answers. In doing so, you'll identify your values and determine which are most important to you. This analysis allows you to focus your energy in creating what you want. Complete the following exercises and then answer the questions that follow.

Personal Values

What's important to you?

You have 100 points to distribute throughout the following list of values. You must use up all 100 points, giving the highest number of points to items that are most important to you. Once you have completed the distribution, analyze your results with the questions that follow.

Points

1. Recognition (feeling of being admired or respected) _____
2. Power (control over others) _____
3. Pleasure (enjoyment) _____
4. Wealth (material possession) _____
5. Independence (freedom, autonomy) _____
6. Health (concern for one's body) _____
7. Intellectual stimulation (looking for knowledge) _____
8. Achievement (accomplishment, expertise) _____
9. Humanitarianism (service to others) _____
10. Religion (faith, conviction, beliefs) _____
11. Politics (contribution to the world) _____
12. Emotional happiness (contentment, peace of mind) _____
13. Creativity (ability to produce something) _____
14. Friendship (close relationships) _____
15. Wisdom (understanding and good sense) _____
16. Aesthetics and nature (love of beauty or outdoors) _____
17. Education (learning) _____
18. Love (affection, intimacy) _____
19. Justice (fairness) _____
20. Equality (an equal chance for all) _____
21. Other (specify): _____ _____

Work Values

What's important to you?

The following list describes a wide variety of satisfactions that people obtain from their jobs. Read the definitions of these satisfactions and rate their degree of importance to you. Use the point scale below. Add any satisfactions not listed but which are of major significance to you.

1 = *Very important in my choice of career*

2 = *Reasonably important*

3 = *Not very important*

4 = *Not important at all*

_____ **Helping society**: Doing something to contribute to the betterment of the world in which I live.

_____ **Helping others:** Being involved in helping other folks in a direct way, either individually or in small groups.

_____ **Public contact:** Having a lot of day-to-day contact with people.

_____ **Working with others**: Having close working relationships with a group; working as a team toward common goals.

_____ **Affiliation:** Being recognized as a member of a particular organization.

_____ **Friendships:** Developing close personal relationships with people as a result of my work activities.

_____ **Competition:** Engaging in activities that pit my abilities against others where there are clear win/lose outcomes.

_____ **Making decisions:** Having the power to decide courses of action, policies, etc.

_____ **Working under pressure:** Working in situations where time pressure is prevalent and/or the quality of my work is judged critically by supervisors, customers, or others.

_____ **Power and authority**: Having control over the work activities or (partially) the destiny of other people.

_____ **Influencing people:** Being in a position to change attitudes or opinions of other people.

_____ **Working alone:** Doing projects by myself, without any significant amount of contact with others.

_____ **Knowledge:** Engaging myself in the pursuit of knowledge, truth, and understanding.

_____ **Intellectual status:** Being regarded as a person of high intellectual prowess or as one who is an acknowledged "expert" in a given field.

_____ **Creativity (artistic):** Engaging in creative work in any of several art forms.

_____ **Creativity (general):** Creating new ideas, programs, organizational structures, or anything else not following a format previously developed by others.

_____ **Aesthetics:** Studying or appreciating the beauty of things, ideas, etc.

_____ **Supervision:** Having a job in which I am directly responsible for the work done by others.

_____ **Change and variety:** Having work responsibilities that frequently change in their content and setting.

_____ **Precision work:** Working in situations where there is very little tolerance for error.

_____ **Stability:** Having a work routine and job duties that are largely predictable and not likely to change over a long period of time.

_____ **Security:** Being assured of keeping my job and of a reasonable financial reward.

_____ **Fast pace:** Working in circumstances where there is a high pace of activity, and where work must be done rapidly.

_____ **Recognition:** Being recognized for the quality of my work in some visible or public way.

_____ **Excitement:** Experiencing a high degree of (or frequent) excitement in the course of my work.

_____ **Adventure:** Having work duties that involve frequent risk taking.

_____ **Profit/gain:** Having a strong likelihood of accumulating large amounts of money or other material gain.

_____ **Independence:** Being able to determine the nature of my work without significant direction from others; not having to do what others tell me to do.

_____ **Moral fulfillment:** Feeling that my work is contributing significantly to a set of moral standards that I feel are very important.

_____ **Location:** Finding a place to live (e.g., town, geographical area) that is conducive to my lifestyle and which affords me the opportunity to do the things I most enjoy.

_____ **Community**: Living in a town or city where I can get involved in community affairs.

_____ **Physical challenge:** Having a job that makes physical demands of me that I would find rewarding.

_____ **Time freedom:** Having work responsibilities that I can work on according to my own time schedule; no specific working hours required.

_____ **OTHER SATISFACTIONS (SPECIFY):**

Review your responses and answer the following questions.

Personal Values

1.   What about your ratings surprised you?

2.   What additional personal values did you identify that were not included in the list?

3.   What were the top five qualities in order of priority?

        a.

        b.

        c.

        d.

        e.

4. What were the bottom five qualities in order of priority?

    a.

    b.

    c.

    d.

    e.

Work Values

1. What additional work values did you identify that were not included in the list?

2. How do your personal values relate to your work values?

3. Based on the values you identified, what conclusions can you make about your career choices?

4. Did you discover anything new about yourself?

Chapter 2

Professional Presence

Creating Your Personal Brand

*Don't just express your-
self, invent yourself. And
don't restrict yourself to
off-the-shelf models.*

—Henry Louis Gates, Jr.

- Identify the qualities, characteristics, or traits that make you distinctive from your competitors.

- What is the future benefit model that you offer?

Personal Branding

(How you package yourself internally and externally)

About Branding

Self-promotion and techniques for marketing yourself have been around since ancient times. Many of the concepts presented by Dale Carnegie in the 1930s could be applied to the development of personal branding. Tom Peters's 1997 *Fast Company* article, "The Brand Called You," began the modern era of the personal branding phenomenon. Branding in the marketplace is **similar to branding cattle on the ranch**.

It has been decades since Tom Peters wrote his article, but the advice remains solid:

- **Differentiate your service** from all the other services, and

- **Create the perception** that there is no other service on the market quite like yours.

Instead of identifying yourself with such terms as *employee* or *manager,* you must instead think of yourself in terms such as "CEO of Me, Inc." Everyone brands you—family, friends, politicians, marketers, supervisors, and coworkers. If you don't take control of your brand, you could be stuck with how others judge you and not how you want to be judged. **What do you want people to think when your name is mentioned?**

*Think of yourself as a diamond in the rough needing a
little pressure and heat to shine.*

Personal Branding

- is the concept of defining your work skills and personality in a way that facilitates self-promotion and self-marketing.

- describes the unique features of your service and the process by which you market yourself to others.

- separates you from the competition.

- reinforces the strength of your operation.

- creates a positive image.

- is your reputation—the perception of *you* held by the external world.

- is the art of articulating and communicating your skills, personality, and values so that others seek you to solve a problem.

—Dan Scawbel

It is not enough to be known for what you do.
You must be known for what you do differently
and effectively.

The main outcome of personal branding should be a clear, deep, and profound understanding of who you are, what you stand for, and what you want to be known for.

Elements of Branding

- **Value Proposition:** What do I stand for?

- **Value Differentiation:** What makes me stand out?

- **Value Marketability:** What makes me compelling?

Brand Equity and Depreciation

- Brand **equity** is created when the brand is thoughtfully built, carefully managed, and positive associations are cemented

- Brand **depreciation** occurs when the brand is mismanaged, misunderstood or neglected

You are a brand. You are in charge of your brand. There is no single path to success, and there is no right way to create the brand called YOU.

—Tom Peters

Another Perspective: The Johari Window

- The Johari Window concept is particularly helpful to understanding self-awareness, personal development, and intergroup relations.

- The Johari Window model is also referred to as a disclosure/feedback model of self-awareness. It illustrates the process of giving and receiving feedback.

- The Johari Window model was created by American psychologists Joseph Luft and Harry Ingham in 1955. The model was later expanded by Luft.

- Luft and Ingham called their Johari Window model "Johari" after combining their first names, Joe and Harry.

- Luft and Ingham observed that there are aspects of our personality that we're open about and other elements that we keep to ourselves.

- At the same time, there are things that others see in us that we're not aware of.

- The Johari Window is a four-paned window that divides personal awareness into four different types, as represented by its four quadrants:

1. *Open Quadrant:* What is known by the person about her/himself and is also known by others (behavior, attitude, feelings, emotions, knowledge, skills, views). For example: your name, the color of your eyes, the fact you may have a family or own a pet.

2. *Blind Quadrant:* What is known about a person by others but is unknown by the person. Note it is best to seek feedback from others to reduce this area and thereby increase the open area. For example: your manners, the feelings of other people about you.

3. *Hidden Quadrant:* What is known to ourselves but kept hidden from others. A person may fear that if people knew feelings, perceptions, and opinions, they might reject, attack, or hurt individuals. For example your secrets, your, hopes, desires, what you like or dislike.

4. *Unknown Quadrant:* Unknown to the person and unknown to others. Knowing all about oneself is extremely unlikely. The unknown extension represents the part of you that may always remain unknown (the unconscious in Freudian terms). For example an ability that is underestimated or untried due to lack of opportunity or encouragement, a natural ability or aptitude that a person doesn't realize they possess, conditioned behavior or attitudes from childhood, or a fear or aversion that a person does not know they have.

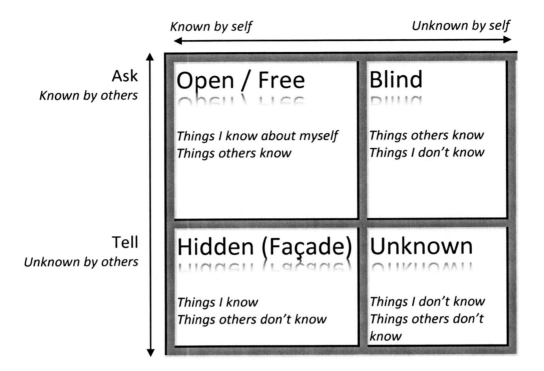

- The lines dividing the four quadrants are like window panes, each of which can move as an interaction progresses.

- The Johari Window panes can be changed in size to reflect the relevant proportions of each type of knowledge of/about a particular person in a given group or team situation.

- The application of the Johari Window comes in opening up the Open Quadrant, thus making the other three areas as small as possible.

- As your levels of confidence and self-esteem develop, you may actively invite others to comment on your blind spots through regular and honest exchange of feedback.

- People around you will understand what "makes you tick" and what you find easy or difficult to do, and will provide appropriate support.

The Brand-Me Strategy

1. **Brand Development**: Determine who you are and what you stand for. Examples: Your values, mission, vision, and the principles that guide you.

2. **Brand Packaging**: Visually and implicitly represent your values, mission, vision, and principles with your professional presence.

   Examples: Your website, business card, office space, personal style, speaking style, dress, and grooming.

3. **Brand Communication**: Mobilize your brand by getting the word out.

   Examples: Networking, volunteering (personal and professional), blogging, writing articles, and random acts of kindness.

Everything you do affects your personal brand. That includes:

- The way you walk, talk, and dress
- Your education and profession
- Your choice of friends, spouse, and business colleagues
- The way you meet your obligations
- Your customer service skills
- How you follow through on your promises

Before you begin the process of identifying your brand, what do you think people think when they see you at work? Identify three or four words that you think should initially pop in their heads.

Are you . . .

helpful	trustworthy	collaborative
flexible	a team player	tactful
a problem solver	creative	insightful
assertive	dependable	determined
an effective communicator	an organizer	friendly
	adaptable	enthusiastic

Are you . . .

inconsistent	arrogant	dramatic
picky	withdrawn	stubborn
cold	aggressive	lazy
passive	nosy	unscrupulous

Just forget about your job description. Think about what makes you different from the other employees. Identify the qualities, characteristics or noteworthy traits that make you distinctive from your competitors, coworkers, and colleagues. What is the future benefit model that your brand offers? How do you want to be perceived?

Do you . . .

- deliver your work on time?

- save your organization money and headaches?

- give your internal and external customers dependable, reliable service that meets their strategic needs?

- anticipate and solve problems before they become crises?

Creating Your Personal Brand

Write down three or four phrases or sentences that represents your brand. Remember your brand should be **authentic**, **consistent**, and **clear**. This is only a first draft—a brand is not built overnight.

1.

2.

3.

4.

Developing a Mission Statement

Your **mission statement** is your personal philosophy or creed. It should focus on what you want to be (character), what you do (contributions and achievements), and what values or principles your being and doing are based on.

- Start by asking yourself questions about what you want to accomplish.

- Always be positive.

- No more than one paragraph, two or three sentences. Keep it simple.

- Include positive behaviors, character traits, and values that are important and want to develop further.

- Review your mission statement at least once a year.

- This statement should guide your daily actions and decisions.

It is my mission to . . .

Examples:

It is my mission to further my knowledge every day of my life to enhance my personal and professional growth.

My mission is to influence my clients with the spirit of progress by continually providing the means, strategies, and products that will help to enhance their net worth, protect their families' security, and help create prosperity in all of their business and private financial endeavors.

Packaging Your Brand

Your Professional Presence

Once you have established who you are, what you are about, and how you want to be perceived, you must then begin to develop the professional presence that identifies your brand. First impressions are very important.

How will you package your brand?

- Facial expressions _____

- E-mails, memos, telephone messages _____

- Cubicle or office setting _____

- Voice (articulation, pitch, pace and tone) _____

- Your blog and website contents _____

- Use of appropriate non-verbals

- Accessories (purses, shoes, jewelry, briefcases, pens, and notebooks)

- Your handshake

- Dress and grooming

Your image puts a framework around all your credentials.

While industries have individual dress codes, in most organizations, the rule of thumb is to present no visual surprises. Remember the four *B*s:

No **Boobs**, No **Belly**, No **Back**, No **Butt**.

The Motown Etiquette Coach

Ms. Maxine Powell

Maxine Powell (finishing instructor, consultant, fashion designer) brought refinement and sophistication to many of the most gifted popular music artists in the 1960s. A founding member of Motown's Artist Development department, Powell became the record company's finishing instructor as well as fashion designer and consultant from 1964 to 1969. She stressed the importance of social etiquette, posture, and stage presence. Her personal instruction helped launch the careers of artists such as Smokey Robinson, Martha Reeves, Diana Ross and the Supremes, Marvin Gaye, Stevie Wonder, and the Temptations.

Powell spent two hours a day with each performer, teaching them that they were being trained for two places: The White House and Buckingham Palace. Under Powell's guidance Motown artists were groomed to play the stages of the Copacabana, the Latin Casino, the *Ed Sullivan Show*, and concert halls throughout England. She taught positive change through body language, public speaking, appropriate clothing, and etiquette.

To quote Martha Reeves, "Powell taught the Motown performers that each individual was capable of achieving an intrinsic sense of beauty. She told us we were all God's flowers and inspired us to let the inner being show."

Workplace Fashion Tips

Always Dress to Impress

- When in doubt, dress conservatively. Err on the side of being too formal.

- Wear minimal jewelry.

- Don't wear perfumes or cologne.

- Cover visible tattoos.

- Remove piercing jewelry except for pair of small or moderately sized earrings.

- Choose conservative colors that complement you.

- Stay clear of wild patterns and prints.

Tattoos and Body Piercings

Are They Worth Your Job?

While there is nothing wrong with tattoos and piercings, there also is nothing unlawful about an employer saying, "We don't want body piercings or tattoos." Now considered body art by the youngest generations, tattoos and piercings may seem logical and beautiful to you but may not seem so to others. Just remember that some people (particularly older generations)—maybe your next employer—may see your body art as body mutilation.

Some things to keep in mind about tattoos and piercings:

- Avoid tattoos that could be perceived as vulgar or offensive (no hateful or sexual symbols).

- Be careful where you put them. Are they going to be visible in your work clothes?

- Consider the culture of the organization.

Cube Etiquette 101

Cubicles are now very common in office settings. Many of us work in office cubicles or other open environments. An employee can spend 40 hours per week in a cubicle. However, studies show that most workers are not thrilled with the idea of working in a cube because of the lack of privacy and the increased noise that come with the territory.

Life in a cube presents certain challenges. One of the challenges is how coworkers with different personalities, working styles, preferences, and cultural backgrounds can work successfully in a cubicle environment. Some people are more extraverted and need to talk. Others are introverted and prefer to work all day without interruption; they get their energy from within.

Some people say that cubicles offer more of a psychological than a physical barrier between employee workspaces. It is hard to keep noise, smells, and other disturbances from spilling over the partitions. But if people realize that they must minimize their "spill-over," life in cubicles can be easier and the cubicle workplace can be very productive.

In cubicle environments, common courtesy is more important than ever. A little bit of politeness goes a long way toward avoiding problems. Everybody should model good behavior and expect it in return from their coworkers. Supervisors can play an important role in setting the tone by creating specific policies for healthy office culture and, when necessary, negotiating conflicts between employees.

Here are some ways you can exercise proper cubicle etiquette and make your work environment more conducive to getting work done.

Privacy

- Conceptualize invisible walls and doors. Do not talk or holler over the top of your cubicle.

- Never enter someone's cubicle without permission. Do not barge in and begin talking. Behave as though cubicles have doors. Do not enter before you have eye-contact "permission" from the occupant.

- Do not sneak up behind someone in a cube. Announce yourself at his or her doorway or lightly knock on the wall.

- Post a sign or flag at your cube entrance to signal when you can be interrupted. Avoid making eye contact with people if you don't want to be interrupted.

- Don't "prairie-dog" over the tops of cubes or peek in as you walk past each one. Keep your eyes straight ahead.

- Don't loiter outside someone's cube while you wait for him or her to finish a phone call. Come back at another time.

- Never read someone else's computer screen or comment on conversations you've overheard. Resist answering a question you overheard asked in the cube next to you!

- Keep your hands off a cube-dweller's desk. Just because there's no door doesn't mean you can help yourself to her paper clips or stapler.

In Your Cube

- Kick others out gracefully. Politely let others know you have work to finish.

- Respect quiet. Think before interrupting someone who appears to be deep in thought.

- Don't discuss confidential or personal information in your cubicle. General Rule: Would you want this information on the Internet or the local news? If not, don't discuss it in your cubicle; find a more private space instead.

- If you are having a break or lunch with someone else, do so in the break room, not in your cubicle.

Phones

- Try to pick up your phone on the first ring. Set the ringer volume at the lowest level you can hear.

- Never use speakerphone in your cubicle. If there is someone else who needs to listen in for a conference call, use a meeting room.

- Watch your volume when talking on the phone. A headset can help keep your voice low. It can also free up your hands to work on the computer while you are talking.

- When you leave your cubicle, turn your phone ringer off and let it go to voicemail or forward your phone number to your cell phone.

- Never leave your cell phone behind in your cube without first turning it off or switching its ringer to vibrate.

- With personal or sensitive calls, be aware that your neighbors can hear your end of the conversation.

- Don't interrupt or stand over people who are taking calls.

Talking

- Use your "library voice." Talk softly; don't shout.

- Don't talk through cube walls or congregate outside someone's cube. For impromptu meetings, go to a conference room or break room.

- Don't bring clients to your cube to meet with them. Go to a closed-off office or conference room.

- Don't yell across the "cube farm." Get up and move to the other person's location.

General Noise

- Use e-mail or instant messaging to communicate silently with your coworkers.

- Use headphones when listening to music. Do not sing, whistle, or hum along.

- Set your computer's volume to a low level and turn off screensaver sound effects.

- Set your cell phone to vibrate.

- Work out an arrangement with your neighbors to take lunch breaks at different times. This will give each of you some quiet time in your cube.

- Eat quietly. Avoid gum-popping, smacking your lips, slurping, and eating crunchy foods.

Smells

- A good general rule is to never eat hot food or strong-smelling foods at your desk. Food odors can bother your hungry or nauseous neighbors. Remember that other people will have to live with those odors all afternoon.

- Perfume and cologne should be avoided in a cubicle arrangement. Your neighbors may have allergies or be more sensitive to fragrances in general.

- Keep a neutralizing air freshener handy.

- Keep your shoes on!

- Keep snacking to a minimum at your desk. As previously mentioned, choose quiet foods to snack on.

Decorations

- Take pride in your work area—it is a reflection of yourself.

- Maintain a clean and tidy workspace.

- Keep decorations simple and inoffensive to others.

- Keep plants clean and trimmed.

- Do not intrude on your coworkers' space with your cubicle plants.

In General

- Remember that your cubicle is the property of your organization, not your personal kingdom.

- Do your grooming at home or in the rest room; for instance, do not floss your teeth or trim your eyebrows, beard, or nails in your cube.

- If you are a cube lunch eater, keep in mind that other people are also "enjoying" your meal with you.

- Don't assume your annoying habits are a secret just because you have some visual privacy. Your coworkers will notice when you chew ice, clip your nails, or tap your pen on your desk.

Communicating Your Brand

Always Challenge Yourself

- Get visibility for what you accomplish. Toot your own horn!

- Continue to learn.

- Volunteer to make professional presentations.

- Develop your professional website.

- Write a professional blog.

- Sign up for extra projects at work.

- Join professional organizations.

- Teach a class on a subject you are passionate about.

- Attend networking sessions.

- Write an article for your organization or local newspaper.

- Perform above the norm.

- Request challenging assignments.

- Develop your "elevator speech."

- Continuously update your resume.

Developing Your Elevator Speech

- An elevator speech is a short, one-to-three word sentence statement that communicates "Why I am someone worth hiring, helping, or working with."

- The idea of an elevator speech is to have a prepared presentation that grabs attention and says a lot in a few words.

- An elevator speech comes in handy when you attend an event, a conference, convention, or some type of meeting with networking opportunities.

- It answers the question "What do you do?"

Do

   ✓ Memorize it—don't ramble.

   ✓ Make it sound effortless, conversational, and natural.

✓ Avoid an elevator speech that will leave the listener mentally asking "So what?"

✓ Maintain eye contact.

✓ Practice, practice, practice!

✓ Focus on how you can benefit the organization or resolve a problem.

✓ Incorporate examples and stories to help support your points.

Weaker Example:

I have spent the last three years in labor relations. My objective is to move to a larger office where I can get more involved in EEO law. I graduated in 2005 from Ohio University.

Stronger Example:

I have three years of labor relations experience with specific expertise in union relations, classification, and employee grievances. In my current position, I developed a classification methodology that was adopted by the entire organization and saves us an estimated $1 million annually. I graduated in 2005 from Ohio University as a joint law and human resources development major.

Elevator Speech

Create a draft of your Elevator Speech, then try it out with someone you trust to give you honest feedback. Then, revise and repeat.

Putting It All Together

1. What factors contribute most to your self-esteem?

2. What are your most important values? How do they apply to your work?

3. What is your mission statement?

4. What are your passions (things you love to do)?

5. What do you consider to be your greatest professional accomplishment so far?

6. What are your top brand attributes?

7. Who is your competition in the marketplace and what differentiates you from them?

8. What would your supervisor say are your most positive attributes?

9. What would you most like to be remembered for on your job?

10. What are your top goals for improving your professional presence for the next year or two?

Chapter 3
Networking
Make Your Contacts Count

*Networks are people talking to
each other, sharing ideas, information, and resources. . . .*
Networking *is a verb, not a noun.*
—John Naisbitt, *Masters of Networking*

Networking is an organized method of making links from people you know to the people they know, gaining and using an ever-expanding base of contacts. Networking is an opportunity to help advance your career and develop yourself. Networking is about who knows you and your capabilities, not who you know.

Note that it is not called *netjive* or *netsit* or *neteat;* it is *network*. In order to be a successful networker, you need to "work" the network. Networking means sharing, saying "thank you," and keeping your word.

Networking skills involve communicating and listening.

- Learn about the people you meet.

- Identify what needs you can help fulfill.

- Match the needs of one person with the needs of another (sometimes your own).

Identifying Your Networks

Work/ Business	Professional	Social	Family/ Extended	Friends/ Inner Circle	Other
Coworkers Clients/Customers Fellow commuters	Fellow members of professional groups	Twitter Facebook LinkedIn	Siblings Mother of your sister-in-law	Classmates Friends of friends	Sports Cultural groups Religious groups Teachers

Levels of Networking

According to Lynn Waymon, there are six levels of networking, ranging from mere accidents of meeting to the establishment of strong allies (Baber & Waymon, 2007). In understanding these levels, you can assess your current network, decide where to put your energies to widen and deepen your network, and see what to do and say to have more of a networking relationship with others.

Waymon's six networking types are:

1. **Accidents:** People you will never see again under normal circumstances

2. **Acquaintances:** People you have met through other contacts, but have an area in common

3. **Associates:** People with whom you share a membership (civic group, fitness group, professional association, soccer parent, etc.)

4. **Actors:** People who actively exchange information and resources with you

5. **Advocates:** People who send opportunities your way, speak up for you, and promote you

6. **Allies:** People who are invested in your life-long business and personal success and who can give you constructive criticism, commiserate with you, and celebrate with you.

> ## *Introducing Yourself*
>
> When introducing yourself, remember:
>
> - Firm handshake
>
> - Direct eye contact (U.S.)
>
> - Give your first and last name
>
> - Look at the person's name tag (especially if you're a visual learner)

Decide What You Have to Give

To create an active networking resource, give something.

—Baber & Waymon (2007)

Remember to develop active networking relationship with others. To move from Associate to Actor, you must be willing to give.

You have a lot to give!

enthusiasm	tips	businesses
discoveries	shortcuts	expertise
resources	support	ideas
reviews	new products	trends
referrals	services	

What do you want to . . .

find?	connect with?	be aware of?
solve?	discover?	have more of in your life?
investigate?	brainstorm?	
learn more about?	do more often?	

Networking Suggestions

- Before you go to an event where you are networking, prepare an agenda (what you have to give and what you want to get). Put it on Post-it note or an index card and review just before attending the function.

- If the event serves refreshments, do not overeat or overdrink.

- Maintain an approachable facial expression and stance.

- Prepare your introduction to others beforehand: name, position, and agency or business affiliation.

- Your introduction should be composed of one sentence about what you do best and one sentence that provides a testimonial, a vivid example.

- Follow up via e-mail, personal note, and/or telephone, even with those you do not believe can help you right now.

- Make offers to help others. You are there to contribute as well as benefit.

- Do not cluster with your friends. Should you find you have become a part of a cluster, assert yourself and suggest you all move out and circulate.

- Invest 3 to 5 minutes with one person before moving on.

- When it is time to move on, don't lie with "I'll be right back" when you do not intend to return. Be tactful and direct: "I've enjoyed speaking with you. Thank you for your time. There a few more people I would like to talk with. In case we don't reconnect tonight, perhaps we can catch up within the next couple of weeks."

- Do approach higher-ranked individuals and introduce yourself.

- If name badges are provided, be sure to wear yours high and to your right. Do not clip your badge on your breast or down by your belt buckle.

- Remember: networking is not the same as selling.

- Be sensitive to names—linger longer.

"What Do You Do?"

Create a Two-Part Answer

When asked what you do, create a specific, positive concept of yourself doing what you want to be known for.

1.   Tell what you want someone to remember about you, what you want to be known for (refer to Johari Window concept).

2.   Give a specific example that shows how you solved a problem, saved the day, or served the client or customer. Keep in mind that people will remember the stories you tell more easily than your title or occupation.

What do you want your contact to know about you? Once you figure this out, you will know what to say.

Small Talk Is Smart Talk

Small talk can be annoying or intimidating if approached in the wrong way. But at its best, small talk can help establish rapport and lead to richer conversation. Here are some key tips to keep in mind when engaging in small talk:

- Don't tell all (broken refrigerator)

- Use the word "you" more than "I"

- Ask questions about the other person

- Feel confident that you have something to contribute to the conversation

Small-Talk Topics

- Sports

- Weather/climate

- Travel

- Arts, media, books

- Hobbies

- Pets

- Birthplace

Topics to Avoid

- Death

- Politics

- Religion

- Sex

- Vulgar or insensitive jokes and expressions

If You're Bad With Names

Some of us have a hard time remembering names. To avoid appearing rude or unattentive, try these tricks during an introduction:

- Repeat the first name or confirm the last name.

- Ask the person to spell her or his name.

- Mentally associate the name with a visual.

- Ask how the person got his or her name.

- Say the person's name again as you leave.

Your Networking Opportunities

Develop a list of opportunities you may have to network—then make them work for you.

1.

2.

3.

4.

5.

Chapter 4
Political Savvy

*Being politically savvy does not
mean you have to sell your soul!*

Office politics: Events that increase or decrease a person's power and advantage in an organizational setting.

Office politics are played to obtain power—the ability to control people or resources, or to get others to do things you want done. Understand that office politics are omnipresent; they are everywhere, all the time.

People who understand and use office politics to their advantage are much likely to succeed than their politically naïve counterparts. Therefore, to gain a competitive edge you need more political skill and knowledge. To ignore office politics is to ignore those underlying forces that account for the success between equally talented people.

Many individuals naturally develop their political savvy unconsciously over their career. For those individuals savvy skills are just considered common sense. However, what is commonsense to the intuitively savvy is actually uncommon sense for others.

At one time, it was assumed that office politics were played primarily by supervisors and managers who were attempting to climb the ladder of success, and by executives who were still either climbing or trying to maintain power. Not only are office politics tougher today, but the stakes are at their highest. In an era of corporate takeovers, downsizings, mergers, and organizations trimming down to reduce costs, the use of political savvy is needed now more than ever for survival.

We all know about devious office politics:

- Back stabbing
- Taking undue credit
- Spying on coworkers
- Discrediting your rival coworkers
- Character assassination
- Snubbing
- Snitching to management
- Faking a romantic involvement
- Lying or covering the truth
- Playing dishonest games
- Discounting another's opinion or idea

Why People Practice Politics

Security Issues

- Scarcity of resources
- Competitive work environment
- Subjective performance standards

Self-Esteem Issues

- Hunger for acceptance
- Emotional insecurity

Power and Influence Issues

- Cravings for power
- Machiavellian tendencies toward people
- Imitating power-holders
- Self-interest

However, it is very naïve to think that all office politics are destructive and unethical. If you define office politics in a narrow way as manipulative, you can overlook the value of political awareness and skill.

To be successful in today's evolving workplace, you need talent, hard work, good job performance, a share of good breaks, and political savvy. *Political savvy* means ethical use of office politics to your advantage. To some, office politics means deceit, deception, and selfishness. However, you should think of political savvy as the ability to practice sensible and ethical office politics.

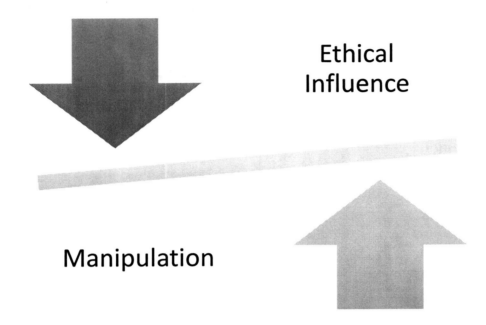

So, What Is Political Savvy?

- Applying subtle and informal **ethical methods** of gaining power or a **competitive edge**.

- The totality of skills for successfully navigating the political dynamics of an organization to accomplish one's goals.

- The **ability to understand what you can and cannot control**, when to take action, who is going to resist your agenda, and whom you need to get on your side.

- Mapping out the political terrain and getting others to take sides, as well as leading coalitions.

The use of tact and diplomacy is very important.

- Tact: the sense of what to say and do without giving offense; knowing what is appropriate and tasteful

- Diplomacy: the skill of negotiating and handling people so that there is no ill will

"Tact and Diplomacy is telling someone to go to hell and they look forward to the trip."

For some people it means "keeping your mouth shut."

"Don't be a broken refrigerator—You can't keep a thing."

When You Would Rather Not Say

- Use humor

- Don't feel obligated to share every detail

- Stay quiet about sensitive matters

Where Do You Stand?

Are you a **Mac**?

- The term *mac* refers to the word *machiavellian*: the view that politics is amoral and that any means, however unscrupulous, can justifiably be used in achieving political power

- Behavior characterized by unscrupulous cunning, deceptions

- Usually identified as a power-hungry, power-grabbing, unscrupulous individual

- Perceived by others as ruthless, devious, and power-crazed

Are you a **Politico**?

- Shrewd maneuverer; someone who typically lands on both feet when deposed from a particular situation

- Has a developed sense of morality and ethics

- Usually shrewd, but not in strong danger of being ruthless

Are you a **Survivalist**?

- Practice enough office politics to take advantage of good opportunities

- Concerned about not making any obvious political blunders such as upstaging the boss in a meeting

- Practice just enough office politics to keep out of trouble with your boss and management

Are you an **Innocent Lamb**?

- No desire for playing politics and seizing power

- Believes that good people are rewarded for their efforts and thus rise to the top

- Only political strategy is "by my works you will know me"

- Keeps eyes focused on the task at hand, hoping that someday hard work will be rewarded

- *Has no clue of what is going on!*

To the totally politically unsavvy, politics in any form is inherently immoral and thus they refuse to take part. The politically unsavvy do not really see the extent to which informal influence is occurring behind the scenes. They believe that their organization and their own behaviors are highly rational and that technical merit alone suffices to sway decisions. Many people have political blind spots where they cannot consciously see the extent to which informal influence shapes the decision-making process.

The truth is…

At the lowest level of office politics at the survivalist level, you can engage in several activities without considering yourself a "political person." For example:

- Relationship building

- Networking

- Team involvement

- Persuasive communications

- Information gathering

- Maintaining emotional self-control

Political savvy has little to do with one's place in the hierarchy—all employees can use political savvy regardless of their position in the organization.

Characteristics of a Politically Savvy Individual

- Chooses to become an active, ethical player

- Believes in and cares about the issue at hand

- Plays above board

- Legitimizes the task; avoids the political blind spot

- Uses power to get things done

- Spreads the credit

- Is an effective team player

- Promotes self but not at the expense of others

Basic Power-Acquiring Tactics

- Develop your expertise

- Form alliances with powerful people

- Think, act, and look powerful

- Develop a network of useful contacts

- Squeeze power out of a committee assignment

- Acquire seniority

- Collect and use IOUs

- Find a champion or mentor

- Be visible

- Perform deliberate acts of kindness

- Listen and pretend your microphone is always on

- Establish boundaries of conversation and relationships

- Use tact and diplomacy

- Be flexible—be able to go with the flow

- Be willing to listen to and understand other view points

> ## The Power Perch
>
> - In meetings, the head of the table is the "power perch."
>
> - Other important positions are the seats immediately to the right or left of the power perch and the seat opposite the power perch (unless it's too far away).
>
> - Round tables blur status at meetings.

To successfully manage office politics, the savvy must:

- Be able to quickly assess situations to determine who holds power and who is faking.

- Develop appropriate political self-defense strategies.

- Identify politically dangerous situations and effectively avoid committing political blunders.

What Can You Do?

- Perform deliberate acts of kindness
- Pretend your microphone is always on
- Establish boundaries of conversation and relationships
- Be flexible
- Be willing to listen to and understand other view points
- Chart out your course (your personal Individual Development Plan)
- See the world through your boss's eyes
- Pay attention to your professional image
- Always challenge yourself
  - Attend networking sessions
  - Write a professional blog or website
  - Volunteer to make professional presentations
  - Sign up for extra projects at work
  - Join professional organizations
- Extend your radar
  - Read newspapers, books, and other publications with comprehensive political analyses (several available online)
  - Expose yourself to opposing viewpoints on particular issues
  - Tune in to radio and TV programs that cover political issues
  - Serve on a community outreach program
  - Arrange a detail or shadow assignment in a legislator's office
  - Learn who has the power (formal and informal)
  - Identify friends and foes
  - Network
  - Start small
  - Find a champion or mentor

Cultivating the Support of Higher-Decision Makers

1. Shine at meetings
   - Appear articulate, poised, and successful
   - Ask set-up questions
   - Allow others to talk
   - Take notes when influential people speak

2. Show that you can identify with top management

3. Appear cool under pressure

4. Show an interest in your organization and its mission

5. Contact and/or welcome newly arrived office holders

6. Don't criticize pet projects of the top players

7. Display business manners and etiquette
   - Respect people's senses
   - Show class at lunch and meals
   - Remember names
   - Make appointments to talk with high-ranking people (never try to just drop in)
   - Use tact and diplomacy

8. Get your name in front of influential people
   - Send copies of memos of your significant achievement
   - Associate yourself with a special project, major committee, and/or task force

9. Get your hands dirty before the right audience—be willing to do menial work in a pinch to get the job done

---

Clever Insults Over the Ages...

When Insults Were an Art Form

"He has no enemies but he is intensely disliked by his friends."
—Oscar Wilde

"I have never killed a man, but I have read many obituaries with great pleasure."
—Clarence Darrow

"I didn't attend his funeral, but I sent a nice letter saying I approved of it." —Mark Twain

"He is a self-made man and worships his creator." —John Bright

Influencing Your Supervisor

Impressing your supervisor is the most basic strategy of office politics.

1. Check out the chemistry between you and your supervisor

2. Understand your supervisor

    • Find out your boss's true objectives

    • Figure out if your supervisor is a reader or a listener

    • Understand "boss" language

3. Support your supervisor

4. Help your supervisor succeed

5. Avoid upstaging your supervisor

6. Reward your supervisor

7. Share your accomplishments with your supervisor

8. Avoid drama

9. Show loyalty

10. Teach your supervisor a new skill

11. Know when to engage in small talk

Gaining Support of Coworkers

1. Be a team player

   - Be supportive of others

   - Share the credit

   - Make use of humor

   - Share information

   - Touch base with coworkers before presenting ideas

2. Ask for advice

3. Exchange favors

4. Express sincere interest in colleagues' work, families, and hobbies

5. Store up a reservoir of good feelings

   - Be a good listener

   - Do not snoop

   - Do not spread malicious gossip

6. Be a firefighter (problem solver)

7. Become a center for provisions—be a "go-to" person

8. Use appropriate compliments

- More effective to compliment a person's actions than a person's traits and characteristics
- Individualize; do not use the same compliment for everyone

9. Make a good showing at the office socials

- Avoid talking shop excessively
- Read the newspaper before going
- Look like you are having fun
- Practice smiling before you go
- Engage in sports in a noncompetitive, friendly way
- Identify people you want to meet

Topics You May Not Want to Share With All Your Coworkers

- Wild weekends, hangovers
- Off-color jokes or comments centered on racial, ethnic, or gender themes
- Financial information
- Medical history
- Lifestyle changes
- People gossip
- Political and religious views
- Workplace complaints
- Personal problems, intimate details of your love life
- Social networking profiles and personal blogs

Workplace Socials

The Politically Savvy understand the importance of workplace socials. Attending workplace socials can be an opportunity to:

- Show that you are a team player
- Network
- Meet important people in your organization
- Understand the culture of the organization

Political Savvy No-Nos

- Not showing up. You may leave early, but you need to attend.
- Missing the "big moment" (the reason for the event)
- Eating over the buffet or asking for a plate to take home
- Ignoring your boss
- Surprising your boss
- Bypassing your boss
- Upstaging your boss
- Being disloyal
- Clustering with your friends
- Getting too familiar or flirting with others
- Being aggressive (I win, you lose)
- Getting drunk, high, or buzzed
- Being obnoxious or negative
- Burning your bridges
- Deviating too far from organizational culture

What Do You Know?

Information and analysis are powerful! The more you know, the better you can position yourself for success. The following section will help you assess what you already know, and don't, about your organization, supervisor, coworkers, and employees.

A fundamental part of political savvy is knowing how your organization, supervisor, employees, and coworkers operate. Answer the following questions and then reflect.

What Do You Know About Your Organization?

- Who is the CEO, director, secretary, commander, or president of the organization, and what do you know about him or her? Identify the leadership qualities attributed to this individual.

- Who is second in command and what do you know about him or her? Identify the leadership qualities associated with this individual.

- What are your organization's top three work priorities?

- What is the mission of the organization/agency?

- What is the vision of the organization?

- How does your organization generate information (memos, formal meetings, phone calls, informal meetings, e-mails, texting, other)?

- What is the preferred style of working?

    _____ Very organized and highly structured

    _____ Moderately organized and structured

    _____ Little organization or structure

- Is the organization

    _____ Present-oriented?

    _____ Future-oriented?

- Identify the outside groups that lobby for your organization.

- Identify the outside groups that lobby against your organization.

- Identify the champions in congress for your organization.

- How is the budget for your organization appropriated?

In the space below, reflect on what you have written.

What Do You Know About Your Supervisor?

- What are your supervisor's top three work priorities?

- How does your supervisor prefer to receive information (memos, formal meetings, phone calls, informal meetings, e-mails, texting, other)?

- What is your supervisor's preferred style of working?

  _____ Very organized and highly structured

  _____ Moderately organized and structured

  _____ Little organization or structure

- Is your supervisor

  _____ More introverted (reflects inwardly and prefers quiet time for thinking about things)

  OR

  _____ More extroverted (reflects outwardly and prefers talking about things with others)?

- Is your supervisor

  _____ A big-picture person?

  _____ A detail person?

- Is your supervisor

  _____ Past-oriented?

  _____ Present-oriented?

  _____ Future-oriented?

- What is your supervisor's primary conflict style?

  _____ *Competitive* (assertive and uncooperative)—pursues own concerns at others' expense

  _____ *Accommodating* (unassertive and cooperative)—neglects own concerns to satisfy the concerns of others

  _____ *Avoidant* (unassertive and uncooperative)—does not immediately pursue own concerns or those of the other person

_____ *Collaborative* (assertive and cooperative)—attempts to work with the other person to find solutions that fully satisfy the concerns of both parties

_____ *Compromising* (intermediate in both assertive and cooperativeness)—attempts to find some expedient, mutually acceptable solution that partially satisfies both parties

- What are your supervisor's three outstanding strengths?

- What are your supervisor's three greatest developmental needs? How are you working with her or him to address those needs?

- What is your supervisor's greatest stressor?

- What do you know about your supervisor's family? Is he or she single, married, or does he or she have a significant other? Any children? Any grandchildren? Mom and dad still living? Any pets?

- What are your supervisor's favorite hobbies, sports, or outside interests?

What Does Your Supervisor Know About You?

- What will your supervisor say are your three greatest strengths?

- What will your supervisor say are your three greatest developmental needs? How are you working with him or her to address those needs?

- Does your supervisor know what you need from him or her to perform your work satisfactorily? If the answer is yes, what are your needs and how did you let your supervisor know of your needs? If the answer is no, why not?

- What does your supervisor know about your family?

- What does your supervisor know about your favorite hobbies, sports, or outside interests?

Now reflect on what you have written. What do you need to do to improve your political savvy?

What Do You Know About Your Coworkers?

- Who are the team players?

- Who are the "drama" people?

- Who is a problem solver?

- Who can you count on in a jam?

- Who are the superstars?

- Who are your adversaries?

- Who are your allies, your advocates?

My Influence Chart

	My Division	Division A	Division B	Division C	Division D
Higher level than me					
Same level as me					
Lower level than me					

Read the questions below, and write your answers in the above grid according to the person's division and level.

- Who are the people you eat lunch with on a regular basis? If you eat lunch with the same people every day and they are all in your office, you probably aren't expanding your sphere of influence.

- Who are two people at work you can trust to give you honest feedback?

- Who are two people are higher than you in the organization, who are willing to meet with you and give you advice and input when you request it?

- Who is the one "go-to" person in each department? There may be more than one for each department.

Review the grid. What did you discover?

Attracting a Mentor

Mentor: A trusted friend, counselor, or teacher; usually a more experienced person.

The ancient Greeks were among the first to use mentoring as a tool for developing talent. Greek mythology provides us with much information on mentoring practices. During the Trojan Wars, Odysseus left his son Telemachus with his friend Mentor who would teach and guide his son in his absence.

Today mentors provide expertise to less experienced individuals to help them advance their careers, enhance their education, and build their networks. In many different arenas people have benefited from being part of a mentoring relationship.

Examples:

- Politicians—Aristotle mentored Alexander the Great

- Business People—Freddie Laker mentored Richard Branson

- Movie Directors—Martin Scorsese mentored Oliver Stone

- Movies—Obi-Wan Kenobi mentored Anakin Skywalker and his son Luke Skywalker.

Today, mentoring is considered a key development tool. A potential mentee can do much to attract a mentor. But first, you must make some decisions.

1. Determine if you need formal mentoring versus informal mentoring (see table on the next page). Many people start with mentors at the informal level and then go into a formal organizational mentoring program.

2. Determine the type of mentoring—Strategic mentoring or tactical mentoring? Note that both are very important.

   Strategic mentoring refers to thinking, planning, and actions that reflect the individual's ability to consider the big picture, recognize patterns and trends, honor priorities, anticipate issues, predict outcomes, and have smart alternatives to fall back upon. Strategic issues deal with over-

Formal Mentoring	*Informal Mentoring*
Defined length of time	Undefined length of time (sometimes years)
Specifically designed	Occurs by chance or designated
Established goals, clarified and shared	Goals and needs determined by individual
Tied to competencies	No accountability
Professional skills development	Personal development
Organizationally driven	Personal chemistry
Structured training	Training identified

riding mission and purpose, why the organization exists, how it makes a difference that others don't or can't make, and where it will be in the future.

Tactical mentoring refers to the hands-on part of getting the job done, making sure the strategic goals are met. It's performing each implementation task with quality and efficiency.

3. Determine how a mentor can help. One of the most valuable things a mentor can do is help you take an honest look at yourself related to strategy and tactics. Don't wait for the ideal mentor; instead, pull key teachings from several.

Suggestions

Identify your goals

- Develop an individual career/life development plan that charts out your career path and life goals

- Talk with your supervisor about your development needs

- Identify formal leadership programs you want to apply to

- Identify specifically what you seek to learn from a mentor

Excel at what you do

- Know your job and go beyond the expected

- Be identified as competent and trustworthy

Be visible

- Volunteer for special projects
- Help others
- Network with others

Learn to take risks

- Sign up for special projects
- Introduce yourself to new people within the organization
- Be prepared to accept feedback

Publicize your achievements

- Write articles for agency, civic groups
- Write a letter to a friend or family member about what you have accomplished in one year
- Take pictures to capture the moment and feeling

Office Gossip

There are two kinds of office gossip: **personal** and **professional**.

- Personal: Gossip about who's dating, divorcing, sleeping around, etc.

- Professional: Gossip about what's going on in the organization, organizational advocates and competitors, the budget, potential mergers, downsizing, who's getting ahead in your field or organization, etc.

You can listen to all of it, but let the personal gossip pass in one ear and out through the other. Professional gossip has importance, so pay attention and keep track of it. This is one way to hone your skills in office politics.

Use political savvy

- Value your reputation
- Choose well—research the reputation of the mentor
- Be perceived as an ethical team player
- Think and plan strategically about how you will reach your goals

Thank-You Notes Using Snail Mail

Thank-you notes are incredibly valuable for establishing professional presence because so few people take the time to write them. A thoughtful thank-you note can improve your professional relationships, and is especially useful:

- after a job interview—to thank the interviewer for their time, and to thank anyone at home or work who helped you get in or through an interview,

- when someone gives you a gift, and

- when someone does a favor for you.

When composing a thank-you note, keep the following in mind.

- Include 1–2 lines about why their assistance or quality was important to you.

- Either hand-write or type and print out. Do not use e-mail!

- Use only dark blue or black ink.

More great tips can be found at www.thankyounotes.com. Following are some examples of successful thank-you notes.

Dear Mr. Jones,

Thank you for meeting with me last Wednesday. I appreciated the opportunity to speak with you about your career within this organization. The insights you provided have helped me create a more realistic career path. Again, thank you for your time.

Sincerely,

Dear Ms. Smith,

Thank you for taking the time to interview me for your upcoming opening in your office. I enjoyed meeting you and learning about the organization. Based on our discussion, I'm sure that I have the qualifications your organization seeks.

Sincerely,

Dear Mr. Johnson,

Thank you for letting me know that the position in your office has been filled. I hope you will keep my resume on file and consider me for a future opening.

Sincerely,

Identifying Your Organizational Culture[1]

1. Who are the super stars or rock stars in your organization and immediate office? What did they do to win admiration of others?

2. Who are the villains or outcasts? What did they do to cause disfavor?

3. What behaviors and characteristics are rewarded?

---

1   Adapted from Terrence E. Deal and Allen A. Kennedy (1982). *Corporate Cultures*. New York, NY: Basic Books.

4. How do people communicate important messages—writing, e-mail, telephone, face-to-face, or a combination?

5. Who is getting ahead? Who is getting promoted?

6. How does the organization's mission influence daily work in your office?

7. How do decisions get made in your office—top down, shared, other?

8. What opportunities do you have for socializing with the people you work with? Are parties or social events part of the culture?

9. Do people come in early and work late?

10. What training programs and opportunities for growth does your office and/or organization support?

Chapter 5
Conflict Management

With Contributions by
Tim Stranges, The Timothy Group

Conflict is an unavoidable part of life. We know that conflict comes in all shapes and sizes, and as long as two or more people are working together somewhere, it will never go away. But if we don't learn to master the art of managing conflict, we will continue to hurt ourselves and others.

- *Conflict management* is a systematic process to find a satisfying outcome between disputing parties. With conflict management, teams, groups, and organizations function more effectively and achieve goals.

- The process of conflict management involves understanding the nature of the conflict and who is involved, and then initiating resolution.

- If you dread confrontation, chances are you could be paying a heavy price at the expense of your career success and personal happiness.

- Note that many methods intended for addressing conflict in groups might also be effective in addressing conflict between two people.

- If the process of conflict management is viewed as an opportunity for growth and change in a work environment, the potential for a positive outcome is great. On an individual level, the ability to solve problems and manage change plays an important role in one's success.

How Do You Deal With Conflict?

Conflict is an inevitable part of the human experience. We can deal with it better if we accept it as a natural part of our lives instead of wishing for it to disappear or to never even surface.

You can only control your response to the conflict, not the outcome. Sometimes, people are just difficult and nothing you do will change this reality. In most of these cases there are other forces at play that are beyond your control.

Conflict clearly plays an important role in human interactions. However, it is a double-edged sword. When properly dealt with, conflict can actually yield very positive results.

The Desirability of Conflict

Conflict Can Be Good!

The Value of Conflict:

1. Prevents stagnation

2. Stimulates interest and curiosity

3. Causes personal and social change

4. Provides a medium through which grievances can be aired

5. Resolves tension among individuals

6. Creates new ideas and innovations

Conflict can help eliminate or reduce the likelihood of groupthink. *Groupthink* (a concept developed by Irving Janis) is a way to refer to a mode of thinking that people engage in when they are deeply involved as a cohesive in-group. When group members strive for unanimity, it overrides their motivation to realistically analyze alternative courses of action. Group members often conform in thought and behavior—an unthinking acceptance of majority opinion. The tendency of group members to share common assumptions about their vulnerability frequently leads to mistakes.

Examples of the negative consequences of groupthink are the *Challenger* disaster, the escalation of the Vietnam War, and the Watergate scandal. Groupthink is more fully discussed in chapter 8, "Working in Groups."

Thomas-Kilmann Conflict Styles

One of the first steps in dealing with conflict is to identify your preferred conflict style and learn how to manage a variety of situations using different styles.

Dr. Kenneth Thomas and Dr. Ralph Kilmann (1974) developed a model that identified five common strategies or styles for dealing with conflict. Their basic premise is that individuals tend to have a natural, habitual way of dealing with conflict that takes over when they are under pressure. The habitual way corresponds with one of the five identified conflict MODEs (management of differences exercises).

The styles have two basic dimensions:

- **Assertiveness:** the extent to which the person attempts to satisfy his or her own concerns

- **Cooperativeness**: the extent to which a person attempts to satisfy the concerns of others

These two basic dimensions of behavior define the five different modes for responding to conflict situations: Avoiding, Competing, Collaborating, Accommodating, and Compromising.

Your conflict behavior in the workplace is a result of both your personal predisposition (mode) and the situation in which you find yourself. If you are in a conflict with a coworker, the Thomas-Kilmann chart can help you figure out how to handle the situation. It allows you to see what category best describes your behavior when dealing with conflict and it allows you to examine alternative styles of successfully managing your conflict.

All the styles can be used effectively in the right context, but some styles are poorly suited to certain situations. The key to conflict management is developing the ability to choose the mode that best fits the situation and to increase your level of comfort with the alternative styles.

The following chart identifies the five different modes. One axis of the chart is for measuring how important it is for you to have your needs met (Assertiveness), and the other axis is used for measuring the importance you place on meeting others' needs (Cooperativeness).

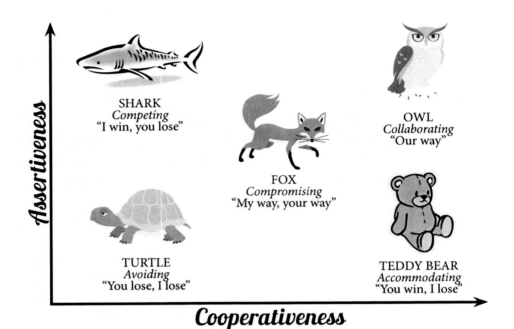

1. **Avoiding (Turtle)**

"You lose, I lose."

"I will think about it tomorrow."

- Lower left corner of the chart
- Both unassertive and uncooperative
- Goal is to delay
- Also known as the flight mode
- Withdraws from a threatening situation
- Neither pursues own concerns nor those of the other individual

2. Competing (Shark)

"I win, you lose."

"My way or the highway."

- Upper left corner of the chart
- High assertion and low cooperativeness
- Power-oriented mode
- Goal to win at all costs
- The individual's aim is to pursue one's agenda at another's expense
- May mean standing up for one's right or defending a cherished position

3. Collaborating (Owl)

"I win, you win."

"Two heads are better than one."

- Upper right corner of the chart
- Both assertive and cooperative
- Goal is to find a win-win situation
- Concerned with finding creative solutions to issues that satisfy both individual's concerns
- Takes time and effort
- Opposite of avoiding

4. Accommodating (Teddy Bear)

"You win, I lose."

"It's OK with me; whatever you want."

- Lower right corner of the chart
- Unassertive and cooperative
- The goal is to yield to another's point of view
- Tends to neglect own needs to satisfy the concerns of others
- Element of self-sacrifice or charity
- May yield to another person's concerns when he or she would prefer not to
- Focuses on preserving the relationship versus attaining goals

5. Compromising (Fox)

"Let's make a deal."

"My way, your way."

- Style in the middle of being assertive and cooperative

- Goal is to find a quick middle ground

- Mode also known as sharing

- May mean splitting the difference between two positions

- Ability to exhibit all of the other animal traits (in small degree) in order to deal with conflict, at least on the superficial level.

Strategically Using the Conflict Styles

All the styles are relevant, useful, and can help you navigate conflict with success when utilized strategically. While we can use all five styles at different times, we tend to prefer one or two habitual styles in conflict situations. The key is to understand when to use which styles.

Style	Useful When . . .	Inappropriate When . . .
Avoiding	• Issues are trivial • There is little chance of satisfaction • Confrontation costs are too high • Delays are advantageous	• Important decisions need to be made • Negative feelings are likely to linger

Competing	• Quick, decisive action is needed • Enforcing discipline • Protection is needed • You know you're right on vital issues	• Respect for others is diminished • It causes too much fear and fighting • It creates "yes men," stifles initiative
Collaborating	• Creative solutions to "enlarge the pie" are possible • Relationships <u>and</u> issues are significant • Reasonable hope exists to meet all concerns	• Time is short • Investment of effort is not worth the outcome
Accommodating	• You realize you are wrong • You think the good will is worth it • You are losing and outmatched • You are allowing others to "try their wings"	• Your needs are not being met • You may harbor resentment • Your skills go unused • You lose self-respect
Compromising	• Other modes require too much effort • Other modes fail • Equal power exists on both sides with mutually exclusive goals • Seeking temporary settlements to complex issues • There are time pressures	• Larger issues are at stake • You can't live with the result • A pattern of "giving up" is created

What Conflict Management Style Should You Use?

Read the following scenarios and decide which of the five conflict styles you should use to have the best outcome. See page 240 for the best approach to each scenario.

1.　　Stella was hired by your boss about three months ago, and she has been an absolute disaster. She is supposed to assist you with your work, but she spends more time trying to get out of work than doing it. She uses her paid time off as soon as she earns it, and she is often late for work. You have had numerous discussions with her alone and with her and your boss together about job expectations and time and attendance. She improves for a day or two, and then reverts back to her old habits. You have confronted her whenever she is late, and she reacts by claiming you are discriminating against her because she is a single mom with a child who is hard to get up in the morning. Then she runs to the boss and tells him how bad you are. On Monday of this week your boss told you in confidence that he is going to fire Stella. When she comes in on Friday morning, he will tell her to clean out her desk and leave. She will get two weeks' severance pay. Stella was on time on Monday and Tuesday, but she was an hour late today.

Which style should you use in dealing with Stella?

2.　　For the last two years you have been working as a recruitment specialist in the Human Resources department of a mid-size company. When you were hired you were told by the president of the company that he wanted you to bring in a more diverse group of applicants. You have been very successful in doing this, but your boss, the Director of Human Resources, always finds something wrong with the well-qualified minorities and women who are brought in for interviews. Nine months ago, he told an applicant in an interview that he thought her accent was too heavy to be understood by customers and coworkers. You were upset that he said that, especially since the applicant had gone to high school in the United States, majored in English at an American university, and spoke with only a slight accent. At the time, you told your boss that his remark had opened the company up to a discrimination complaint; and, sure enough, the woman filed a complaint with the EEOC when she wasn't hired. The company settled with her for a payment of $25,000. Now your boss has done it again. In an interview earlier today, he asked the best-qualified applicant what his religion was and when the applicant responded that he was a Muslim, the boss said he didn't know how the other employees would react to that information. You are appalled by his statement and know that if the applicant is not selected for the position, there will be another discrimination complaint, probably more costly than the last.

Which style should you use in dealing with your boss?

3.   You are the head of the local office of a large international organization. Most of your small staff of 10 employees has worked together ever since the office opened 9 years ago. The lease on your office is up in one year, and you have been told by headquarters that you can either stay in the current space or move anywhere within five miles provided the annual rent does not go up more than 10%. Many of your employees have complained about the office and its surroundings: occasional thefts from the office, frequent mice in the building, costly parking, few restaurants nearby, etc. But a couple of employees really like the location because it's within walking distance of their homes. You want to be able to address the concerns of as many of the employees as you can in determining whether and where to move.

Which style should you use in dealing with your employees?

4.   This summer you hired three interns, all of whom are rising seniors and management majors in college. You gave them an assignment to study workflow in the accounts receivable branch and come up with suggestions on how it could be streamlined. They have spent four weeks studying the current system and researching best practices in other companies, and have now come to you with a proposed new workflow that they would like to pilot with one of the teams in the branch. You know that the team members would like to try something new. You also know that the cost of implementing the new workflow would be minimal, even if it failed. But you are reluctant to try it because a similar system was tried five years ago in another team and it failed miserably.

Which style should you use in dealing with the interns?

5.   It's early March and your boss has asked everyone for their summer vacation plans. You have always taken the first week of August off, when you, your spouse, and your kids rent a condo at the beach just to chill out. You haven't put a deposit on a place for this year yet. Your new coworker has told you that her fiancé's parents always rent several adjacent condos at the beach the first week of August for the extended family, that this is the first year she has been invited, and that she is getting a lot of pressure to go. Your boss has said that you can't both take the same week off, and has asked you to work it out. On the one hand, you would really like to keep your family's little tradition going. On the other, you want to have a good working relationship with your new coworker.

Which style should you use in dealing with your coworker?

A Look at Your Preferred Conflict-Handling Style

The five conflict styles identified by Thomas and Kilmann give insights into how we can successfully manage conflicts using each style appropriately. As explained by Dr. Reginald Adkins (2010),

> We each have our own way of dealing with conflict. The techniques we use are based on many variables such as our basic underlying temperament, our personality, our environment and where we are in our professional career. However, by and large there are five major styles of conflict management techniques in our toolbox. In order to address conflict we draw from collaborating, competing, avoiding, harmonizing or compromising style[s] of management. None of these strategies is superior in and of itself. How effective they are depends on the context in which they are used. (para. 1)

Following is a quick assessment that was adapted from several assessments to help you become more aware of your characteristic approach, or style, in managing conflict. Be sure to answer the questions indicating how you *would* behave rather than how you think you *should* behave. Respond to the statements using the following scale:

1 – *Never*
2 – *Rarely (once in a great while)*

3 – *Sometimes*
4 – *Fairly often*
5 – *Always*

1. I try to negotiate and adopt a give-and-take approach to problem situations.   1 2 3 4 5

2. I try to see conflicts from both sides. What do I need? What does the other person need? What are the issues involved?   1 2 3 4 5

3. I like to win regardless of the costs.   1 2 3 4 5

4. Being in conflict with other people makes me feel uncomfortable and anxious so I keep my mouth shut.   1 2 3 4 5

5. I try to put the needs of others ahead of my own.   1 2 3 4 5

6. Harmony is more important than getting what I want.   1 2 3 4 5

7. I yield to suggestions from others and keep my true opinions to myself to avoid hard feelings.   1 2 3 4 5

8. I am reluctant to admit I am wrong.   1 2 3 4 5

9. I encourage and openly share information with others. My ideas may be just one way to resolve the dispute. Others may have better ideas.   1 2 3 4 5

10. I look for middle ground.   1 2 3 4 5

Note. Adapted from Adkins (2010) and Northouse (2012).

See the scoring guide on page 241 to determine your results.

Principled Negotiation

Negotiating is an often overlooked skill and yet has an enormous impact on our daily professional and personal lives. The reason we negotiate is to produce something better than the results we can obtain without negotiating.

Principled negotiation is a straightforward and universally applicable model for negotiating personal and professional disputes without getting angry or taken advantage of. The terminology was coined in 1981 by Dr. Roger Fisher and Dr. William Ury in their bestselling conflict resolution book, *Getting to Yes*.

The book advocates four fundamental principles of negotiation:

1. Separate the people from the problem;

2. Focus on interests, not positions;

3. Invent options for mutual gain; and

4. Insist on objective criteria.

1. Separate the People From the Problem

Separating the people from the problem means separating relationship issues ("people problems") from substantive issues, and dealing with them independently. People problems tend to involve problems of perception, emotion, and communication.

Perceptions are people's reality; that reality is interpreted differently by different people in different situations. When different parties have different understandings of the dispute, effective negotiation may be very difficult to achieve. People tend to become personally involved with the issues and with their side's positions, so they will tend to interpret critical responses to those issues and positions as personal attacks. Separating the people from the issues allows the parties to address the issues without damaging their personal relationship. It also helps them get a clearer view of the substantive problem.

Suggestions

- Try to see the situation from others' perspectives. You do not have to agree with their perceptions of the situation, but it is important to understand what they think and feel, and why they think and feel as they do.

- Don't try to guess your opponent's intentions based on your own fears. It is common to assume that your opponent plans to do just what you fear they will do.

- Avoid blaming your opponent for the problem. Blame, even if it is deserved, will only make your opponent defensive. Even worse, your opponent may attack you in response. Blame is generally counterproductive.

- Discuss each other's perceptions. Explicit discussion of each side's perceptions will help both sides to better understand each other and avoid projecting their fears.

- Give your opponent a stake in the outcome by making sure they participate in the negotiation process.

For example:

You are a technician in the IT department of your organization. An employee brings in his laptop and complains that he cannot get into it to turn on. You ask him when and how it happened, and he answers, "It just stopped working." You notice that there are recent scratch marks on the laptop and one of the corners seems to be slightly bashed in. You think the employee may have dropped the computer. You have a history of not getting along with this employee; in fact, he logged a complaint with your supervisor about your work. You think the complaint was unfounded. You really don't want to help this employee, but you decide to separate the problem from the person and fix the computer anyway.

2. Focus on Interests, Not Positions.

Negotiating about interests means negotiating about things people actually want and need, not what they *say* they want or need. Often, these are not the same. People tend to take extreme positions that are designed to counter their opponents' positions. If asked why they are taking that position, it often turns out that the underlying reasons of both sides—their true interests and needs—are actually compatible, not mutually exclusive.

A *position* is a stance, and a *compromise* is usually an unhappy medium between stances. An *interest* is the underlying needs and/or desires that draw a person to the negotiating table. Defining a problem in terms of positions means that at least one party will "lose" the dispute. When a problem is defined in terms of the parties' underlying interests, it is often possible to find a solution that satisfies both parties' interests.

Suggestions

- Identify each party's interests regarding the issue at hand. This can be done by asking why they hold the positions they do, and by considering why they don't hold other possible positions.

- Once the parties have identified their interests, discuss them together. If a party wants the other side to take their interests into account, that party must explain their interests clearly.

- Discussions should look forward to the desired solution, rather than looking backward on past events.

- By focusing on interests, disputing parties can more easily fulfill the third principle: inventing options for mutual gain.

For example:

An employee and her coworkers work in a cubicle work environment. It is noisy and from time to time everyone has talked about how the noise interferes with their work. Jim and Joanne work in adjacent cubicles. Jim just arrived in the office and has spent the last ten minutes listening to his voice mail on speaker phone. During that time Joanne had to stop working because she couldn't concentrate.

Jim's position is that he needs to listen to his voice mail in order to do his work. Joanne's position is that she needs quiet in order to do her work. Their common interest is getting work done.

3. Invent Options for Mutual Gain.

Look for alternatives. If you don't know what your alternatives are, you might accept an agreement that is far worse than the one you might have gotten, or reject one that is far better than you might otherwise achieve.

Suggestions

- Conduct a brainstorming session where all ideas are allowed.

- Look for new solutions to the problem that will allow both sides to win.

- Do not just fight over the original position, which assumes that for one side to win, the other side must lose.

For example:

A manager has told his two employees, Dave and Bob, to work out their vacation schedules for the holiday season. His only stipulation is that every day at least one of the two employees must be in the office, except Christmas Day and New Year's Day. For the three years they have worked together, Dave has taken off a few days before and after Christmas to be with his family in Los Angeles, and Bob has taken a few days off before and after New Year's Day to party hearty. But this year, Bob is newly married, and he and his wife want to spend Christmas in Chicago with his wife's family.

Dave and Bob decide to brainstorm some options for mutual gain. They come up with the following ideas:

- *Dave takes the week leading up to Christmas off. Bob takes the week after Christmas off. So, they both get to spend some time with their families around Christmas.*

- *Dave and Bob look over the office records referencing the number of phone calls, e-mails, and visitors they get in the few days before and after Christmas. They discover that in the past three years, they've never gotten more than three phone calls and ten e-mails during this time, and have never had a visitor during this time. They present their case to support closing the office, so neither is forced to rush to his destination before Christmas or rush back to the office after. Both Dave and Bob can travel at their own pace.*

- *They agree to share the responsibility to check office calls and e-mails while they are on leave.*

4. Insist on Objective Criteria.

When interests are directly opposed, the parties should use objective criteria to resolve their differences. A decision based on reasonable standards makes it easier for the parties to agree and preserve their good relationship.

- Criteria can include laws, regulations, policies, and precedents.

- Fair market value, assessed value, and Kelley Blue Book value are also examples of objective criteria.

- Parties may need to take a time out from negotiation to research what objective criteria are applicable to their dispute.

For example:

Sue works for Douglas. Both of them agree that Sue is a good worker and both of them want Sue to stay with the company for a long time. Sue had a pay increase on January 1 and wants another one on July 1, based on the great work she did on the ABC project. Douglas does not want to give her a pay increase, but is willing to put her in for a large cash award. Sue is unhappy; her stance is that her annual salary should be increased. Before going any further with their negotiations, Douglas suggests that they look at the Personnel Manual to find out what the procedures are for mid-year raises. These "objective criteria" state that mid-year raises are not allowed, but that managers can give cash awards up to $7,500 at any time. Based on these criteria, the focus of their negotiations now turns to the size of the cash award.

- In most negotiations, the long-term relationship is far more important than whatever is being negotiated on that day. How many times has a good working relationship been weakened because someone "won" and someone "lost?" Negotiations should be viewed as an opportunity to build and deepen relationships.

- The idea is not to win but to create a solution that will benefit the relationship. At the very minimum the solution should not harm your relationship with the other party.

- Always develop a backup plan if agreement cannot be reached. One never wants to go into a negotiation without a backup plan. Developing a backup plan also helps you to determine your own interests—what's really important to you.

- Try to determine what the backup plan for the other party might be. Do this by examining the other party's interests. By finding out the other party's interests you are better able to meet their needs during negotiation.

Questions to Answer

Adapted from the "Conflict Resolution" resources webpage by Harry Webne-Behrman (n.d.).

1. Which needs of mine are truly threatened by this conflict?

2. What are the needs that are most important to be negotiated at this time?

3. If we are unable or unwilling to negotiate a meaningful agreement, what are my alternatives?

   BATNA (best alternative to a negotiated agreement)

   WATNA (worst alternative to a negotiated agreement)

   MLATNA (most likely alternative to a negotiated agreement)

4. How might these relate to the situation facing the other person(s) involved in this dispute? (Would their analysis be similar or different?)

5. When it really comes down to it, what do I want to happen as a result of this process?

BATNA: Best Alternative to a Negotiated Agreement

- Your BATNA is your alternative plan, especially when the negotiations start to get out of control. It can also be your trump card to either make the negotiation happen to your advantage, or to help you walk away from it altogether.

- "Don't put all your eggs in one basket": This wise old proverb, which has stood the test of time for good reason, warns that if you bring only a single proposal to the table, you may likely end up with a rotten deal or no deal at all. You need to have an alternative plan waiting in the wings.

- Having a good alternative empowers you with the confidence to either reach a mutually satisfactory agreement or walk away to a better alternative. Without a clear idea of your BATNA, you are simply negotiating blindly. The BATNA is also key to making the most of existing assets.

WATNA: Worst Alternative to a Negotiated Agreement

- In a negotiation, your WATNA represents one of several less desirable paths that you can follow if a resolution cannot be reached. Like the BATNA, understanding your WATNA is essential to making informed decisions at the bargaining table.

- The WATNA can be useful in evaluating whether to walk away from an agreement. If the WATNA is better than the proposed resolution on the table, you may be inclined to take the risk and walk away from the mediated agreement.

MLATNA: Most Likely Alternative to a Negotiated Agreement

- Your MLATNA represents the most likely alternative that will happen if you don't reach agreement with the other party.

- Like the BATNA and WATNA, you need to weigh your MLATNA against what is on the table.

- You also need to think about the other party's MLATNA and how it may impact their negotiations.

Let's go back to the example of Sue and Douglas.

Now that Sue knows her boss cannot give her a mid-year raise, but can give her a cash award of up to $7,500, that what she wants: $7,500. Douglas has never given a cash award of more than $4,000, but says he is willing to go up to $5,000 for Sue. His reasoning is that while he wants to recognize her for her great work on the ABC project, he just found out that his entire annual budget for cash awards is only $10,000, and he wants to hold some money in reserve for the rest of the year. He has a couple of employees working on very high-profile projects and doing a great job. He'd like to be able to award them later in the year.

Sue is very upset with Douglas's offer of $5,000, and she starts thinking of her BATNA, WATNA, and MLATNA.

> *Sue's BATNA: Douglas will change his mind and give her the $7,500.*

> *Sue's WATNA: Douglas will be so upset with her attitude, he will change his mind and give her nothing. She will be so mad, she will quit and have no job.*

> *Sue's MLATNA: Douglas will stick with his position and give her $5,000. She will take the $5,000 and quietly start looking for a new position with a higher salary.*

Douglas is thinking about how Sue will react to his offer of $5,000, and he starts thinking of his BATNA, WATNA, and MLATNA.

> *Douglas's BATNA: Sue will thank him for the cash award of $5,000 and continue working at her outstanding level.*

> *Douglas's WATNA: Sue will be so upset about the "stingy" $5,000 award that she will quit, the company will lose an excellent employee, and he will have to do her work until he can hire a replacement.*

> *Douglas's MLATNA: Sue will be upset about the $5,000 award, but won't show it. She will start looking for a new job. Rather than lose her to another company, Douglas will talk with her about opportunities for advancement elsewhere in this company. After all, he can only give her one more raise before she is at the*

top of the salary range for her current position. She is a valuable asset that the company should try to retain.

Negotiation Strategies

Participants are friends	Participants are adversaries	Participants are problem-solvers
The goal is agreement.	The goal is victory.	The goal is a wise outcome reached efficiently and amicably.
Make concessions to cultivate the relationship.	Demand concessions as a condition of the relationship.	Separate the people from the problem.
Be soft on the people and the problem.	Be hard on the people and the problem.	Be soft on the people, hard on the problem.
Trust others.	Distrust others.	Proceed independent of trust.
Change your position easily.	Dig into your position.	Focus on interests, not positions.
Make offers.	Make threats.	Explore interests.
Disclose your bottom line.	Mislead your bottom line.	Avoid having a bottom line.
Accept one-sided losses to reach agreement.	Demand one-sided gains as the price of agreement.	Invent options for mutual gain.
Search for the single answer: the one they will accept.	Search for the single answer: the one you will accept.	Develop multiple options to choose from; decide later.
Insist on agreement.	Insist on your position.	Insist on using objective criteria.
Try to avoid a contest of will.	Try to win a contest of will.	Try to reach a result based on standards independent of will.

A Few Thoughts on Workplace Bullying

Bullying in the workplace is aggressive behavior (I win, you lose). Workplace bullying can include anything from making belittling comments to excluding someone from an important meeting. The work bully sets out on a course of constant but often subtle harassment.

Bullying may involve race, religion, age, gender, disability, or color, all of which are protected criteria under law. However, most workplace hostility occurs simply because someone doesn't like someone else. The problem is that the tactics used by workplace bullies usually are *micro-inequities* (think of them as small paper cuts) and difficult to complain about. It may start with a belittling comment at a staff meeting, an eye roll, a glare, a dismissive snort, or silences. Some supervisors may even condone bullying as part of an office initiation. If the bully is a supervisor, it may be condoned as a tough management style.

Review the following list of behaviors. Think in terms of the behaviors you exhibit toward your coworkers and the behaviors your coworkers exhibit toward you. Occasional insults don't count. Bullying occurs when the behavior has occurred consistently over a long period of time. While some of the behaviors listed may seem trivial, when repeated over and over again they take a psychological toll on the victim.

- Unwanted or invalid criticism
- Blame without factual justification
- Swearing, cursing at the victim
- Glaring in a hostile manner
- Storming out of the work area when the victim enters
- Giving the "silent treatment," ignoring the victim

- Yelling or shouting at the victim in a hostile manner
- Negative comments about the victim's intelligence or competence
- Consistently failing to return the victim's telephone calls or respond to memos or e-mail
- Mean pranks
- Withholding needed information
- Derogatory name-calling
- Rumors or gossip targeted at the victim
- Destroying or needlessly taking resources that are required to do the victim's job
- Throwing temper tantrums when the victim disagrees
- Preventing the victim from expressing him- or herself (e.g., interrupting when speaking)
- Turning other employees against the victim
- Taking credit for the victim's work or ideas
- Reprimanding or "putting down" the victim in front of others

Still, it can be hard sometimes to distinguish between normal personality clashes and the incessant torture that is workplace bullying.

What can you do? Whether the bully is your boss or your coworker, first you must realize that no one should ever make you feel fearful at work. If you are a victim of bullying in your workplace, consider speaking to someone in the human resources department for help in dealing with it. If you would like to try to deal with the situation before you report it, here are some tips:

1. Regain control by

- Acknowledging you are being bullied
- Knowing that you are not the source of the problem
- Recognizing that bullying is about control

2. Take action.

- Seek the advice of a trusted mentor who may have dealt with this situation before.

- If you can, confront the bully in a professional manner, but only if your physical safety isn't threatened. Don't sink to his or her level. Stay as calm as possible. Give direct eye contact. Don't yell or threaten. Often, bullies are looking for this type of confrontation and it will encourage them to come back for more. Try not to cry or show weakness, either; that's usually what the bully is after in the first place.

- Don't try to win over other people to your side.

- Don't allow the bully to intimidate you or make you feel bad about yourself.

- Do your job and do it well. The workplace bully wants you to fail. When you succeed, the bully is defeated.

- Don't allow the bully to isolate you from your colleagues. Keep up your workplace friendships.

 If you are being physically threatened, don't waste a minute before you report it to both your employer and the police.

Inappropriate Use of the Internet

Inappropriate use of the Internet takes the form of:

- inappropriate/offensive e-mails
- electronic threats
- social networking gossip

All can be considered cyber-bullying. According to the National Crime Prevention Council, cyber-bullying occurs "when the Internet, cell phones or other devices are used to send or post text or images intended to hurt or embarrass another person." Cyber-bullying occurs when someone uses information technology to make fun of or repeatedly pick on another person directly (with text messages, e-mail, etc.); or to harm, damage, humiliate, or isolate another person publicly (through online forums, social media, etc.).

Cyber-bullying is a passive form of bullying in that the bully can remain unknown. It is as serious as any other form of workplace harassment. Where workplace bullying usually pits one bully against one target, cyber-bullying can easily take the form of cyber-mobbing where many people come together against one target. All a workplace bully needs to know is your e-mail address or cell phone number. They can remain anonymous under an assumed e-mail identity, or block their number when calling you.

Sometimes coworkers forward e-mails of questionable content such as a joke or comment. If a joke or supposedly funny e-mail is offensive or hurtful to you, take a proactive stance and request these types of e-mails stop. If the messages continue, alert management about the situation.

What experts suggest you can do to curb cyber-bullying or even cyber-mobbing:

- Report it to management and, if necessary, to the proper authorities

- Take steps to block and verify who contacts you in order to gain back some control. Remember, the bully's nature is to try to take your power because they feel they do not have their own. You do not have to give them anything and you have every right to set up these personal boundaries.

- Save e-mails and texts that contain bullying messages; they can serve as evidence later on if needed.

- Don't use your work e-mail address for anything other than work. Set up a different e-mail account for personal use.

- Don't tell online "friends" (the ones you know through social networking sites) your workplace name. It's relatively easy for others to figure out your work e-mail address if they know your name and the company you work for.

- As far as text messaging goes, once you identify a bully's phone number, block it.

Review: Conflict Styles

1. Which style is the most uncooperative and least assertive?

2. Which style is characterized by assertive behavior, yet represents the maximum in cooperation?

3. Which style is totally cooperative but unassertive?

4. Which style is totally assertive and uncooperative?

5. Which style takes the middle ground on assertiveness and cooperation?

6. Which style is least confrontational and ignores or eases over issues?

7. Which style is "must win" at all costs?

8. Which style do you use most frequently at work? Why?

9. Which style do you use the least at work? Why?

Answers can be found on page 242.

Chapter 6
Technology Etiquette

Remember:

The world does not revolve around you!

Most of us are just not that busy and important.

—Lady Dianne

The use of cell phones, tablets, speakerphones, voicemail, e-mail, faxes, and text messages has become a way of life in business. However, the rules of etiquette have not always kept pace with the innovations of technology. This chapter offers some guidelines on technology etiquette.

The world does not revolve around you. Most of us are not as busy or important as we think we are. So, insisting on checking your messages when you are in the company of your supervisor and coworkers is considered disrespectful, rude, and inattentive. You get the idea.

E-Mail Etiquette

E-mail has become the preferred method of communication for many people in business, but if not used properly, it can become hazardous to relationships and careers. E-mail is a silent form of communication. One can neither see you as you say the words nor hear your vocal inflections; the message is contained entirely in the words you choose to write and send. Because the reader misses out on the nuances of your verbal and visual delivery, the results are often miscommunication and misunderstandings.

E-mail quickly provides written information to organizations, but never let the convenience of e-mail overshadow the value of a phone call or a face-to-face meeting. The "human touch" is often missing from our communications and customers and coworkers alike may appreciate the time and effort it took for you to call or stop by. Try doing both at once—send an e-mail, but call as well to give the recipient a "heads up." Sometimes, hearing your message will enhance your recipient's reading of it.

- **E-mail is best used for short, simple, and straightforward information.**

- Before you hit the send button, it's important to proof the content for spelling and grammar mistakes. But it's also important to read the message aloud to check the tone of the message.

- **Don't forget to add "please" and "thank you."** Those two phrases can transform the snippiest of demands into a polite request.

- **Any message longer than about half the computer screen is too long.** If your content is long, consider introducing the subject in a short e-mail and sending the details as an attachment or fax.

- First ask permission before attaching any large files.

- **Assume any message you send is permanent and may likely be forwarded to others.**

- Start with a salutation, for example, "Dear James." Continue to use salutations until the relationship is well established.

- Be concise. No one likes long e-mails.

- Respond to all questions when returning e-mail.

- Do not use e-mail to send trivial, confidential, or sensitive information. Anything truly urgent should be telephoned. Anything sensitive should be hand-delivered.

- Never use e-mail to reprimand someone.

- Never express political or religious opinions via office e-mail.

- Never use office e-mail to send jokes.

> ## What Does Your E-Mail on the Job Say About You?
>
> Do you communicate electronically with grace and style? Or do you type like a grade-school kid using poor grammar with lots of typos, jargon, and incomplete sentences? People will judge you by the e-mail you send.

- Use humor and sarcasm in your e-mails sparingly. Because tone is so easily lost in written communication, recipients may not "get" the joke.

- Use industry or e-mail acronyms, abbreviations, or emoticons sparingly.

- Define your subject in the subject line.

- Use upper- and lowercase letters when writing. Typing in all-caps is usually read as shouting, and typing in all-lowercase is usually seen as lazy.

- Include your complete business contact information in your signature block at the end of your e-mails.

- Separate your personal and professional e-mail addresses.

- Don't use your current work e-mail to apply for jobs.

- Stick to a conservative black font that is not too small.

- Allow 1–2 days for a response. If you need an immediate response, call as well.

- Respond to your incoming e-mails within 24 hours. If you need more time to respond, call or e-mail your recipient to say you are looking into the problem and will get back to him or her ASAP.

Remember: Business e-mails are a tool, and that tool represents you.

Fax Etiquette

- Faxes have the potential for being quite public; they can be read by anyone who happens across them at the machine.

- As with e-mail, be careful never to fax angry or sensitive content.

- If you need to send confidential information via fax, call the recipient and ask that they wait by the machine at their end.

- Do not send thank-you or congratulatory notes, or any kind of inappropriate jokes or pictures.

Instant Messaging and Texting Etiquette

- Turn off your cell phone during meetings and whenever you are requested to do so.

- Ignore incoming text messages when driving. Pull off the road when you absolutely must answer a message.

- Do not answer text messages while walking—you'll walk into somebody or something.

- Do not put your cell phone on the table during meetings or at restaurants (it's disrespectful to the people you are with, and you might forget it when you leave).

- Do not answer unimportant personal messages in meetings.

- Do not answer messages during meetings unless the message is related to the meeting.

- With instant messaging and texting in business, be careful who's on your buddy list.

- Do not instant message someone who you know is busy, like someone driving a car or in a meeting.

- Do not walk into a conversation with another person if you're texting someone.

Cell Phone Etiquette

- If you must have your cell phone on during meetings, switch to a silent ringer and check your messages only during breaks.

- Speak softly. Keep your voice down to a reasonable level. Cell phones are usually more sound-sensitive than regular phones, so you don't need to yell to make yourself heard—and no amount of shouting will improve a bad connection.

- If you are discussing sensitive or confidential information, remember to talk in an area out of earshot of other listeners.

- When using your cell phone in public buildings, be aware of restrictions against cell phone use and be sure to respect them.

- Inform others at the beginning of a meeting that you are expecting an important call and get their permission to answer it.

- Except in emergencies, do not interrupt a face-to-face conversation to take a cell-phone call. The person you are actually with takes priority. If you have a phone conversation in front of that person, you're showing that he or she is unimportant to you.

- Do not wear your earpiece when not on the phone. This is not unlike being on the phone and carrying on another conversation with someone who is physically in your presence. No one knows if you are here or there.

- Respect the personal space of others by taking your conversation 10 or more feet away from people. Ideally, take your phone call into a private space. Refrain from using your phone in a place where others can't escape your conversation, such as in an elevator or on public transit.

- Keep private matters private. Nobody wants to hear you fight with your spouse or friend over your cell phone. When you use the phone for business, you could leak company-confidential information when talking in public.

Telephone Etiquette

- Answer incoming calls quickly, identifying yourself by first and last name.

- Identify yourself whenever you place a call: first and last name, organization, and nature of call.

- Speak slowly and clearly.

- Listen attentively and add verbal agreement.

- Use honorifics: Mr., Ms., Dr., Sir, Ma'am.

- Return messages within 24 hours.

- If you're in someone else's office or cubicle when they get a phone call, offer to step outside.

- Don't take any calls when someone is in your office unless it's urgent.

- Don't talk to anyone else while you're on the phone.

- Don't do any other work or eat while on the phone.

- If you need place someone on hold, ask the other party if they are able to hold. Never keep someone on hold for longer than a minute. When you return, thank them for holding.

Voicemail Etiquette

- Your outgoing message should be brief, courteous, and include your name, title and company name.

- Keep your outgoing voicemail message current. Update it frequently.

- When out of town, indicate in your message when you'll be back, whether you'll be checking in for messages, how to contact you, or whom to contact in your absence.

- When leaving voicemail for others give your name slowly with proper spelling, company name, and phone number. Briefly specify the purpose of your call. Let them know the best time to reach you. Leave your name and phone number again at the end of the message.

- Tell the person what time you can be reached. For example, "I'll be in my office after four o'clock on Tuesday, Wednesday, and Thursday. Please try to call me at that time on any of those days. I look forward to hearing from you then."

- Leave your name and telephone number at the beginning and end of the voicemail message; that way, people do not have to play back the message. If they did not get your name and telephone number at the beginning, they can get it at the end.

- Try not to ramble when leaving voicemail. Messages should be no longer than 30 seconds.

- If you create some sense of urgency in the call, give a good time for people to reach you. You will increase the chances of people returning your calls rather than dismissing them.

Speakerphone Etiquette

- Use speakerphones sparingly and never use a speakerphone when you are in a cubicle.

- Whenever you use a speakerphone, always ask the other party's permission to do so and identify everyone in the room with you.

- During conference calls, participants should identify themselves whenever speaking.

Check Your E-Mail Address...

It Could Hurt Your Career!

- Unprofessional e-mail addresses can hurt your reputation just as much as unprofessional e-mails.

- It is important to use an address that says something about your personal brand that is professional, inoffensive, and noticeable.

- Separate your personal and professional e-mail addresses.

- Avoid sexual and religious references.

- Never use your current work e-mail address to apply for new jobs.

Techno Communication

Medium	Usefulness	Notes
Formal meeting (Face-to-Face)	• Discussing issues in person with preplanned agenda • Interviewing • Giving team updates (team-building) • Coaching employees • Discussing performance appraisals • Investigating difficult • Giving mentoring sessions • Counseling employees/difficult conversations with employees/coworkers	

Medium	Usefulness	Notes
Brief ad-hoc meeting	<ul><li>Discussing issues that have just arisen and need urgent attention</li><li>Discussing a hot topic that has evoked strong emotion</li><li>Team emergency situations of limited time</li><li>Giving informal briefings</li><li>Announcing achievements (i.e., compliments, awards of employees)</li></ul>	
Phone call	<ul><li>Addressing issues promptly that can be dealt with verbally</li><li>Establishing initial customer contact or beginning a business relationship</li><li>Conference calling to share information with one or more people</li><li>Personal reminding as backup when e-mail is not answered</li><li>Giving information in lieu of e-mail for a complex issue that would require a series of e-mails</li></ul>	
Memo/letter	<ul><li>Acting as a personal reminder</li><li>Explaining why a document has been sent</li><li>Documenting actions taken</li><li>Making a point for the record</li><li>Giving complex work assignments</li><li>Relating important organizational changes</li><li>Giving thank you and appreciations</li></ul>	

Medium	Usefulness	Notes
E-mail	• Giving detailed information that can be printed out as an attachment (i.e. instructions, meeting notes) • Sharing general and mass information that is not too time sensitive. i.e. occur in a few days time or longer • Acting as a reminder for announcement • Giving simple work assignments • Asking for clarification • Giving periodic updates or simple status reports on assignments or request • Giving brief reminders	• More formal than a text message but not quite as formal as a memo • Individual must have time to read and reply
Texting	• Addressing short non-urgent questions • Giving quick and simple information that requires no explanation • Communicating simple yes or no answers • Simple reminders • Checking someone's location	• Texting is limited—way too much can be lost in all the abbreviated text

Now, review this table and identify what types of communication are most appropriate for your workplace and colleagues.

Remember technology devices are only tools; they can never take the place of face-to-face contact.

Chapter 7
Working in Groups

With Contributions by
Bernard Robinson, C.M.C., Institute for Human Development

Most of us have worked in groups during our lifetime. Our early experiences with groups may have been the Boy Scouts or Girl Scouts, a church, or an athletic, social, or fraternal group. In the workplace, at one time or another most of us are required to work in a group and have an idea of their advantages and disadvantages.

Group Synergy

You may have also heard that "the whole is greater than the sum of its parts," and "two heads (or more) are better than one." Both phrases refer to the concept of group synergy. Simply put, groups are often capable of producing higher-quality work and making better decisions than an individual could working alone.

People vary in their need to belong in groups. Some people prefer to work by themselves. Others find being part of a group gives them satisfaction. Whatever our individual needs, we must learn how to successfully work in groups. The fact is that working in a group can meet many of our interpersonal needs. William

Schutz, psychologist and pioneer of the human potential movement, identified three interpersonal needs met by joining groups: inclusion, control, and affection.

1. **Inclusion** is the need to establish identity with others.

2. **Control** is the need to exercise leadership and prove one's abilities. Groups provide outlets for this need. Some individuals do not want to be a leader. For them, groups provide the necessary control over aspects of their lives.

3. **Affection** is the need to develop relationships with people. Groups are an excellent way to make friends and establish relationships.

Group or Team?

**Do you work in a *Group* or on a *Team*?
There is a big difference!**

According to Webster's Dictionary, a *group* is defined as a number of persons considered a collective unit. A *team* is defined as a group of people working together. A richer definition of *team* is a group of people with a high degree of interdependence and who are committed to achieving a common set of objectives, who work well together and who produce high-quality results.

Groups vs. Teams

Put a check (✓) by those that apply to your present work situation.

Groups	Teams
☐ Members think they are grouped together for administrative purposes only. Individuals work independently at cross-purposes with others.	☐ Members recognize their interdependence and understand that personal and team goals are best accomplished with mutual support.
☐ Time is wasted. Members tend to focus on themselves because they are not sufficiently involved in planning the unit objectives. They approach their jobs simply as hired hands.	☐ Time is not wasted struggling over "turf" or attempting personal gain at the expense of others. Members feel a sense of ownership for their jobs and unit because they are committed to goals they helped establish.

☐ Members are told what to do rather than being asked what the best approach would be. Suggestions are not encouraged.

☐ Members distrust the motives of colleagues because they do not understand the role of other members. Expressions of opinion or disagreement are considered divisive or non-supportive.

☐ Members are so cautious about what they say that real understanding is not possible. Game playing may occur and communication traps may be set to catch the unwary.

☐ Members may receive good training but are limited in applying it to the job by the supervisor or other group members.

☐ Members find themselves in conflict situations they do not know how to resolve. Their supervisor may put off intervention until serious damage is done.

☐ Members may or may not participate in decisions affecting the team. Conformity often appears more important than positive results.

☐ Members contribute to the organization's success by applying their unique talents and knowledge to team objectives.

☐ Members work in a climate of trust and are encouraged to express ideas, opinions, disagreements, and feelings. Questions are welcomed.

☐ Members practice open and honest communication. They make an effort to understand each other's point of view.

☐ Members are encouraged to develop skills and apply what they learn on the job. They receive the support of the team.

☐ Members recognize conflict is a normal aspect of human interaction but they view such situation as an opportunity for new ideas and creativity. They work to resolve conflict quickly and constructively.

☐ Members participate in decisions affecting the team but understand their leader must sometimes make a final ruling. Positive results, not conformity, is the goal.

Stages in Group Development

There is a clear pattern of development that groups go through to become fully effective and productive. In 1965 Dr. Bruce W. Tuckman, an educational  psychologist, first described the (then) four distinct stages of development that groups go through to become teams and suggested they need to experience all four stages before they achieve maximum effectiveness. With Mary Ann Jensen, he refined the model in 1977 with the addition of a fifth stage, and it is still one of the most useful and widely used models today.

Understanding and recognizing these patterns contribute to realistic expectations of group behavior. Appropriate behaviors facilitate group development and encourage members to work through their problems. Recognize that the inability to function in one stage sometimes indicates unresolved issues in the previous stage.

The five stages of development identified are: **forming, storming, norming, performing,** and **adjourning.**

Stage 1: Forming

Establishment of some minimal social relationship

In this initial stage the members meet one another and begin defining their roles in the group, exploring their relationship with one another as group members, and sharing ideas about how the group will operate. They are wondering, "How do I belong?" or "What will my role in the group be?" Even if the group members already know each other, the forming stage still occurs if they are just beginning to work on the team. This stage is generally characterized by uncertainty, tentative sharing of information and ideas, polite exploration of options, and careful scrutiny of other members of the team.

Individual behavior is driven by a desire to be accepted by the others and to avoid controversy or conflict. Serious issues and feelings are avoided, and people focus on task-related behaviors and being busy with routines, such as team organization, who does what, when to meet, and so on. But individuals are also gathering information and impressions about each other and about the scope of the task and how to approach it. This is a comfortable stage to be in, but the avoidance of conflict means that not much actually gets done.

Characteristics:

- Individual-centered
- High apprehension; guarded

- Hidden agendas

- Surface politeness; goal to minimize tension

- Lack of structure

Behaviors:

- Most vocal members will dominate

- Feelings and opinions kept hidden

- Inability to stay focused on a task

- High distortion of what is heard

- Lots of voting

- Conflicts suppressed or smoothed over

For Individual Members: How to Get Through the Forming Stage

1. Start to get to know the other group members

   - Introduce yourself

   - Spend time talking with other members of the group

2. Actively participate in establishing ground rules
3. Practice your interpersonal communication skills
4. Actively listen for feelings

Stage 2: Storming

Emergence of some form of conflict

In this second stage, members of the team begin to understand their differences and encounter divergent ideas about their task, their roles, and the processes by which they will do their work.

The central theme of this stage is, "Who's in charge here?" Issues of power and control are characteristic. This stage is generally characterized by disharmony: competition among individuals, ideas, and approaches; conflict among members about differences; frustration about the lack of cohesion; sectionalizing of the team into differing camps; and, threat of the group breaking down. Individuals wonder, "Can I get my ideas across? Will I be able to influence others? Who will be against me?" This is considered a critical stage. Conflicts need to be managed effectively or a team gets stuck at this point and is in danger of not being able to move on to the more productive stages.

Individuals in the group can only remain nice to each other for so long, as important issues start to be addressed. Some people's patience will break early, and minor confrontations will arise that are quickly dealt with or glossed over. These may relate to the work of the group itself, or to roles and responsibilities within the group. Some will observe that it's good to be getting into the real issues, while others will wish to remain in the comfort and security of stage 1. Depending on the culture of the organization and individuals, the conflict will be more or less suppressed—but it'll be there, under the surface. To deal with the conflict, individuals may feel they are winning or losing battles and will look for structural clarity and rules to prevent the conflict persisting.

Characteristics:

- Sense of feeling stuck
- Resistance to structure
- Leadership challenged
- "Outsiders" blamed for any failures
- Infighting and subgroups
- Personal attacks used—defensive reaction to tension

Behaviors:

- Judgmental comments
- Defensive reactions mostly through negative nonverbal behavior

- Unsolicited comments and opinions
- Members opt out
- Absenteeism and tardiness increase
- Team problems discussed outside meetings

For Employees: How to Get Through the Storming Stage

1. Deal with differences in a timely and open manner
2. Be transparent
3. Don't share confidentialities
4. Address behaviors; don't attack team members or their motives
5. Separate the people from the problem
6. Adhere to the ground rules

Stage 3: Norming

Group cohesiveness begins to emerge

In this stage the members of the team recognize and adhere to a common interest in the team and its task, develop common goals for the team, clarify roles of individuals within the team, and develop strategies for working together smoothly. This stage is generally characterized by optimism, deepening of relationships, easing of tensions, resolution of concerns, and the clarification of the team's task and process. Dissent may still exist but attitudes are gradually being modified. Opposing coalitions are dissipating. This is often because the group has begun to accept that the common goal is owned collectively by them and the other members of the team. The group is finding productive ways to deal with conflict, working out issues. The formation of a strong team is underway.

As Stage 3 evolves, the rules of engagement for the group become established, and the scope of the group's tasks or responsibilities is clear and agreed upon. Having had their disagreements, they now understand each other better, and can appreciate each other's skills and experience. Individuals listen to each other, appreciate and support each other, and are prepared to change preconceived views; they feel they're part of a cohesive, effective group.

However, individuals have had to work hard to attain this stage, and may resist any pressure to change—especially from the outside—for fear that the group will break up or revert to the storming phase.

Characteristics:

- More leader-centered; members look to leader to ease tension
- Individuals feel a sense of belonging
- Structure issues resolved
- Issues, not people, are confronted
- Task focus increases
- Complacency may develop

Behaviors:

- Values, assumptions, and opinions openly discussed
- Relevant questions asked
- Willingness to experiment
- Increased willingness to give each other process feedback
- Performance improvement activities undertaken
- More balance in participation

For Employees: How to Get Through the Norming Stage

- Keep the goal in mind
- Share information
- Help others

Stage 4: Performing

Maximization of productivity and consensus

In this stage the members of the team work productively to achieve their goals and carry out their work. This stage is generally characterized by high levels of productivity. A sense of progress and achievement develops, bonds are formed between members, and enthusiasm and creativity levels are high. The ability to reach consensus is achieved and there is a spirit of unity within the group. There is a warmer, more informal climate and a close working relationship among group members. Work is produced in a timely and thorough manner.

Not all groups reach this stage, which is characterized by a state of interdependence and flexibility. Everyone knows each other well enough to be able to work together, and trusts each other enough to allow independent activity. Roles and responsibilities change according to need in an almost seamless way. Group identity, loyalty, and morale are all high, and everyone is equally task- and people-oriented. This high degree of comfort means that all the energy of the group can be directed toward the task(s) at hand.

Characteristics:

- Purpose-centered
- Outside help/resources welcomed
- High trust levels
- Frequent review of process issues
- Team self-corrects, embraces tension as a sign of commitment
- Genuine enjoyment

Behaviors:

- Members reinforce each other verbally and nonverbally
- Willingness to use each other as observers of process and welcome feedback

- Closeness with each other extends outside of meetings

- High levels of role flexibility

- Easy laughter

- Members energize each other

Employees: How to Get Through the Performing Stage

- Spread the credit for success

- Keep the channels of communication open

- Creating and participating in group activities

- Celebrate as a team

Stage 5: Adjourning

Dissolution of the team

In this final stage members of temporarily established teams, having completed their task, prepare to disband. This stage is generally characterized by reluctance to part. Team members review their experiences together, evaluate their accomplishments, and often arrange to keep in touch. For standing teams, especially if they are small, this phase occurs when a member leaves the team.

This stage is about completion and disengagement, both from the tasks and the group members. Individuals will be proud of having achieved so much and glad to have been part of such an enjoyable group. They need to recognize what they've done, and consciously move on. Some authors describe stage 5 as "Deforming and Mourning," recognizing the sense of loss felt by group members.

The basis for healthy group development is trust. Without trust, a group will never reach the fourth stage, at least at the optimal level. When trust is broken, a developed group may need to begin the entire process again. As people join and leave a work group, as the work itself changes, and as organizational policies shift, a group may need to cycle through the process again, perhaps at a different level.

Employees: How to Get Through the Adjourning Stage

- Help your teammates understand their value by contributing to, supporting, and recognizing their accomplishments.

- Personally say good-bye to your teammates.

The stages simply describe the way all groups evolve, whether they are conscious of it or not. But the real value is in recognizing where a group is in the process, and helping it to move to the Performing Stage. In reality, groups are often forming and changing, and each time that happens, they can move to a different stage. A group might be happily Norming or Performing, but a new member might force them back into Storming. It is important for the group to get back to Performing as quickly as possible. Many work groups live in the comfort of Norming, and are fearful of moving backward into Storming, or forward into Performing. This will govern their behavior toward each other, and especially their reaction to change.

Stages	*Individual "I" Needs*	*Group "We" Needs*	*Tasks "Group" Needs*
Forming	Members seek inclusion	Members seek identity	Team seeks definition/clarity of purpose and tasks
Storming	Members seek safety and personal effectiveness	Members tend to freeze-flight-fight	Team seeks effective actions and progress
Norming	Members seek to build trust	Members seek to establish harmony, ground rules and expectations	Teams seeks to clarify vision, mission and goals
Performing	Members define and accept roles	Members engage in collaboration	Teams is working effectively in accomplishing tasks

Adjourning	Members experience separation anxiety and relief	Members achieve a sense of accomplishment sand experience loss of group identity	Team achieves task completion, goal attainment

Ingredients of an Effective Team

- Trust

- Commitment

- Involvement

- Precise objectives

- Open communication

- Emphasis on members' strengths, not weaknesses

- Ownership, collective responsibility

- Creativity

- Conflict management

- Skill development and application

Characteristics of an Effective Team

Clear purpose
The vision, mission, goal, or task of the team has been defined and is now accepted by everyone. There is an action plan.

Informality
The climate tends to be informal, comfortable, and relaxed. There are no obvious tensions or signs of boredom.

Participation
There is much discussion and everyone is encouraged to participate.

Listening
The members use effective listening techniques such as questioning, paraphrasing, and summarizing to get out ideas.

Civilized disagreement
There is disagreement, but the team is comfortable with this and shows no signs of avoiding, smoothing over, or suppressing conflict.

Consensus decision
Important decisions are made by substantial, but not necessarily unanimous, agreement through open discussions of everyone's ideas, avoidance of formal voting, or easy compromises.

Open communication
Team members feel free to express their feelings on tasks as well as on the group's operation. There are few hidden agendas, if any. Communication takes place outside of meetings.

Clear roles and work assignments
There are clear expectations about the roles played by each team member. When action is taken, clear assignments are made, accepted, and carried out. Work is fairly distributed among team members.

Shared leadership
While the team has a formal leader, leadership functions shift from time to time depending upon the circumstances, the needs of the group, and the skills of its members. The formal leader models the appropriate behavior and helps establish positive norms.

External relations	The team spends time developing key outside relationships, mobilizing resources, and building credibility with important players in other parts of the organization.
Style diversity	The team has a broad spectrum of team-player types including members who emphasize attention to task, set goals, focus on process, and question how the team is functioning.
Self-assessment	Periodically, the team stops to examine how well it is functioning and what may be interfering with its effectiveness.

The Importance of Followership

"He that cannot obey cannot command."

—Benjamin Franklin

While followership is written about with less frequency than leadership, it is just as important. Regardless of our position in an organization, whether we like to admit it or not, we all play the role of follower much of the time.

A follower is a person who follows the leadership of another; but a follower is also much more than that. Followership actually represents an interaction that occurs when subordinates work concurrently with leaders toward an organizational goal.

Interestingly, effective followers share many of the same characteristics as effective leaders. As a result, cultivating followership skills can be an excellent way to become a more effective leader. Followership can also be called "leading up," "managing up," or "leading from the middle."

Effective followers are

- Active listeners
- Critical thinkers
- Problem solvers

- Good at working with others
- Understanding of and reflective about goals of the organization

Independent Followership

- Implies the role of flexibility required of both an effective leader and an effective follower.
- The ability to both take over and lead when the situation demands or follow the lead of others when that role is more appropriate.

Laws of Teamwork[1]

The Law of Significance	1 is too small a number to achieve greatness.
The Law of the Big Picture	The goal is more important than the role.
The Law of the Niche	All players have a place where they add the most.
The Law of Mount Everest	As the challenge escalates, the need for teamwork elevates.
The Law of the Chain	The strength of the team is impacted by its weakest link.
The Law of the Compass	Vision gives team members direction and confidence.
The Law of the Bad Apple	Rotten attitudes ruin a team.
The Law of Countability	Teammates must be able to count on each other when it counts.
The Law of Identity	Shared values define the team.
The Law of Communication	Interaction fuels action.
The Law of the Edge	The difference between two equally talented teams is leadership.
The Law of Dividends	Investment in the team compounds over time.

---

1   Adapted from John C. Maxwell, (2001), *The 17 Indisputable Laws of Teamwork: Embrace Them and Empower Your Team.* Nashville, TN: Thomas Nelson.

Developing Trust Behaviors

In his book *The Speed of Trust*, Steven Covey (2006) identifies two things that drive trust: character and competence. In developing trust in relationships, Covey states it is all about consistent behaviors. In every relationship (personal and professional) what you do has far greater impact than anything you say. Thirteen behaviors are identified that are common to high-trust leaders and people worldwide. These thirteen behaviors require a combination of both character and competence. The first five flow initially from character, the second five from competence, and the last three from an almost equal mix of character and competence. Any of these behaviors taken to the extreme, however, do not build trust; and the opposite, or "counterfeit," of each behavior creates the biggest withdrawals of trust.

Character-Based Behaviors

Behavior	*Characteristics*	*Counterfeit*
Behavior #1 **Talk Straight**	• Being honest • Letting people know where you stand • Using simple language • Demonstrating integrity • Calling things what they are	• Withholding information • Giving insincere flattery • Twisting the truth • Manipulating people • Distorting facts • Leaving false impressions
Behavior #2 **Demonstrate Respect**	• Genuinely caring for others • Treating everyone with respect, especially those who can't do anything for you • Showing kindness in the little things • Respecting the dignity of every person and every role	• Faking respect or concern • Showing respect and concern only for those who can do something for you

Behavior #3 **Create Transparency**	• Telling the truth in a way people can verify • Being real and genuine • Erring on the side of disclosure • Being open and authentic	• Having hidden agendas • Saying one thing and doing another for your advantage • Pretending things are different than they really are
Behavior #4 **Right Wrongs**	• Making things right when you are wrong • Apologizing quickly • Making restitution when possible • Not covering things up or letting pride get in the way of doing the right thing	• Covering up mistakes • Denying or justifying wrongs
Behavior #5 **Show Loyalty**	• Giving credit freely • Acknowledging the contributions of others • Speaking about people as if they are present • Representing others who aren't there to speak for themselves • Demonstrating personal humility	• Badmouthing people behind their backs • Disclosing others' private information • Appearing to share credit but then downplaying others' contributions when they are away

Competence-Based Behaviors

	Characteristics	*Counterfeit*
Behavior #6 **Deliver Results**	• Establishing a track record of results • Getting the right things done • Making things happen • Accomplishing what you were hired to do	• Over-promising and under-delivering • Making excuses for not delivering

Behavior #7 Get Better	• Continuously improving • Increasing your capabilities • Being a constant learner • Developing both informal and formal feedback systems • Requesting and thanking people for feedback	• Learning but never producing • Considering yourself above feedback • Assuming today's knowledge and skills will be sufficient for tomorrow's challenges
Behavior #8 Confront Reality	• Taking issues head-on, even the most uncomfortable ones • Addressing the tough stuff directly • Acknowledging the unsaid • Leading out courageously in conversation.	• Avoiding the real issues • Burying your head in the sand
Behavior #9 Clarify Expectations	• Disclosing expectations • Discussing and validating expectations • Renegotiating expectations if needed and possible	• Being vague about specifics • Violating expectations • Assuming that your expectations are always clear and shared
Behavior #10 Practice Accountability	• Holding yourself and others accountable • Taking responsibility for results • Being clear on how you'll communicate, how you're doing, and how others are doing	• Shirking responsibility • Blaming others or finger-pointing when things go wrong

Character and Competence Behaviors

	Characteristics	*Counterfeit*
Behavior #11 **Listen First**	• Listening before you speak • Understanding • Diagnosing • Listening with your ears, eyes, and heart • Finding out what the most important behaviors are to the people you're working with	• Assuming you know what matters most to others • Presuming you have all the answers—or all the questions
Behavior #12 **Keep Commitments**	• Doing what you've said you're going to do • Making commitments carefully and keeping them	• Breaking confidences • Attempting to con your way out of a commitment you've broken
Behavior #13 **Extend Trust**	• Demonstrating a propensity to trust • Extending trust abundantly to those who have earned it • Conditionally extending trust to those who are still earning it • Learning to appropriately extend trust to others based on the situation, risk, and credibility (character and competence) of the people involved	• Withholding trust • Extending false trust by giving people responsibility, but no authority or resources to complete a task • Following up behind people • Micromanaging

Now go back and put a check (✓) by the characteristics you need to work on to successfully work in a group.

Role Flexibility

Can you assume different roles in helping the group move forward?

For groups to be effective, the members must pay attention to both the task and relationship.

- A *group task* is the work the group is trying to get done, the objective of the group.

- A *relationship* task refers to the group's level of trust, openness and cohesiveness.

Research shows that if a group fails to pay attention to either dimension, it fails to do its best work. Research also shows that certain behaviors increase the chance the group will relate in cohesive ways and the chance of the group successfully accomplishing the task.

Some of the most important behaviors are described below. As you review them, analyze your roles in the groups you are part of.

Group Task Roles

Group task roles are directed toward accomplishing the group's objectives through the facilitation of problem-solving.

- **Initiating and contributing**: Proposing new ideas or a change, responding

- **Information seeking and giving**: Giving and asking for clarification and facts

- **Opinion seeking and giving**: Stating and asking about beliefs or opinions related to the issue

- **Elaborating**: Expanding on suggestions

- **Energizing:** Stimulating the group to action or decision

- **Problem solving:** Offering solutions, summarizing decisions, testing for group agreement

- **Assisting**: Helping or facilitating group movement by doing things for the group, for example, performing routine tasks such as distributing materials, rearranging seating

- **Recording**: Writing down suggestions, recording group decisions, or recording the outcomes of the discussion

- **Managing**: Sharing leadership appropriately, using group time well, evaluating performance

Group-Building and Maintenance Roles

Group-building and maintenance roles help the interpersonal functioning of the group. They strengthen, regulate, and perpetuate the group.

- **Listening:** Attending to others, not interrupting

- **Encouraging:** Showing interest in, praising, agreeing with, and accepting others

- **Harmonizing:** Mediating the differences among the other members, attempting to reconcile disagreements, and/or relieving tension in moments of conflict through the use of humor; yielding when necessary to achieve group objectives

- **Compromising:** Within a conflict situation, yielding status, admitting mistakes, disciplining oneself for the sake of group harmony, or coming halfway toward another person

- **Gatekeeping and Expediting:** Attempting to keep communication channels open by encouraging the participation of some or by curbing the participation of others; testing for group satisfaction with the process

- **Observing:** Keeping a record of various aspects of group process and feeding this information, along with interpretations, into the group's evaluation of its procedure by request of group

- **Following:** Going along with the group, accepting the ideas of others, and/or serving as an audience for a group discussion

The most important basic group behavior is common courtesy, and one of the more valued traits for building strong relationships is gratitude.

Individual Roles to Avoid

Individual roles are designed to satisfy an individual's need rather than to contribute to the needs of the group.

- **Aggressing:** Deflating the status of others, disapproving ideas or values of others, attacking the group, joking maliciously

- **Blocking:** Resisting, disagreeing, and opposing beyond reason; bringing up a dead issue after it has been rejected

- **Recognition Seeking:** Calling attention to oneself through boasting, reporting on personal achievements, acting in inappropriate ways or fighting

- **Self-Confessing:** Using the group as an opportunity to express personal non-related feelings, insights, and ideologies

- **Minimal Involvement**: Showing a lack of involvement in the group's task; displaying nonchalance, cynicism, goofing off

- **Dominating:** Trying to assert authority or superiority by manipulating

- **Help Seeking:** Attempting to get sympathy from other group member through expressions of insecurity, personal inadequacy, or self-criticism beyond reason

- **Special-Interest Pleading:** Speaking on behalf of some other group for one's momentary need

Social Styles

Don't expect to work on a team where everyone is totally compatible. Think in terms of members' social styles. *Social style* incorporates a person's personality type, common behavior patterns, and main approach to others.

People who concentrate on . . .	*Tend to . . .*	*Approach this kind of teammate by . . .*
Results	drive self and others to quick, tangible, and measurable results.	giving straight answers.
Accuracy	always think, analyze forces, and consider events.	explaining your reasoning.
Interaction	communicate ideas and feelings openly and expressively.	listening and openly expressing your underlying thoughts.
Harmony	act agreeable, supportive, and cooperative, and smooth over their feelings.	being polite and positive.

Note. Adapted from Pokras, S. (2007). *Working in Teams: A Member Guidebook*, p. 10.

Each style has value and is necessary for effective teamwork. Aim to understand your teammates' styles and approach each teammate accordingly.

Your Team's Social Styles

Team member	Preferred style	Backup styles	Best approach
Me			

Beware of Groupthink

What Is Groupthink?

Groupthink, a term coined by social psychologist Irving Janis (1972), occurs when a group makes faulty decisions because of group pressures. Groupthink occurs when groups are highly cohesive and when they are under considerable pressure to make a quality decision, and often quickly. When pressures for unanimity seem overwhelming, members are less motivated to realistically appraise the alternative courses of action available to them. These group pressures lead to carelessness and irrational thinking, because groups experiencing groupthink fail to consider all alternatives and seek to maintain unanimity. Decisions shaped by groupthink have low probability of achieving the most successful outcomes.

Examples of groupthink "fiascoes" studied by Janis include the United States' failures to anticipate the attack on Pearl Harbor, the Bay of Pigs invasion, the escalation of Vietnam War, and the ill-fated hostage rescue in Iran.

Some negative outcomes of groupthink include:

- Examining few alternatives
- Not being critical of each other's ideas
- Not examining early alternatives
- Not seeking expert opinion
- Being highly selective in gathering information
- Not having contingency plans

Symptoms of Groupthink

- **Illusion of invulnerability:** Members are excessively optimistic, encouraging them to take extreme risks.

- **Collective rationalization:** Members discount warnings and do not reconsider their assumptions.

- **Belief in inherent morality:** Members believe in the rightness of their cause and therefore ignore the ethical or moral consequences of their decisions.

- **Stereotyped views of out-groups:** Negative views of the "enemy" make effective responses to conflict seem unnecessary.

- **Direct pressure on dissenters:** Members are under pressure not to express arguments against any of the group's views.

- **Self-censorship:** Doubts and deviations from the perceived group consensus are not expressed.

- **Illusion of unanimity:** The majority view and judgments are assumed to be unanimous.

- **Self-appointed "mindguards":** Members protect the group and the leader from information that is problematic or contradictory to the group's cohesiveness, view, and/or decisions.

When the above symptoms exist in a group that is trying to make a decision, there is a heightened chance that groupthink will happen.

Remedies for Groupthink

Experts have determined that groupthink may be prevented by adopting some of the following measures:

- Using a policy-forming group that reports to the larger group

- Having leaders remain impartial

- Using different policy groups for different tasks

- Dividing into groups and then discussing differences

- Discussing within sub-groups and then reporting back

- Using outside experts

- Appointing a "devil's advocate" to question all the group's ideas

- Holding a "second-chance meeting" to offer one last opportunity to choose another course of action

Consensus

Consensus is the group's ability to make decisions in which everyone participates and that everyone can support. Reaching a consensus *is* an achievement. It takes work and usually requires time. It can be useful when there's a problem, question, or task that needs everyone's full support. Groups that make decisions by consensus are more committed to their plans and do a better job of making them happen.

Consensus helps everyone be more respectful and understanding toward others.

However, consensus is *not*:

- **Steamrolling.** The 600-pound-gorilla approach to decision making may work, but discussion is suppressed and people almost certainly won't support an outcome reached this way.

- **Voting.** In voting, participants in discussions may be cut short, affecting the quality of the decision, and several members may not support the outcome if they have lost.

- **Trading Off.** "You can have your idea on the list if I can have one of mine"; this kind of compromise may seem efficient, but not all members may support the outcome.

- **Withdrawing.** It may seem to help keep the peace, but it keeps good ideas from being heard, allows some members to not hold themselves accountable, and ultimately prohibits full participation.

- **Perfect Agreement.** Consensus decisions represent what each member of the group has contributed to, can live with, and can support. This is not the same as perfect agreement.

- **Easy or Fast.** Consensus is difficult and taked time (front-loaded time, that is!), but is worth the effort when quality, commitment, and public support of a decision are important.

Basic Consensus Rules

- Express beliefs and ideas clearly and honestly.

- Encourage others to express their ideas.

- Listen carefully to all ideas.

- Allow a time of silence between speakers to reflect on the ideas.

- Work with your team and team leader for the best solution.

- Summarize accurately what you hear.

- Be committed to keeping the tension level among group members to a minimum.

What Can You Do to Ensure the Success of the Team?

- Take time to listen to your teammates.

- Get to know your teammates.

- Be involved in the process and sort out responsibilities and roles (whether official or not).

- Keep an open mind.

- Realize teamwork takes patience and understanding.

- Show respect.

- Support others.

- Understand your role and own it.

- Be a problem solver, rather than sitting back and complaining.

- Keep communication open.

True or False Quiz

1. T   F   Teamwork requires that you get to know your teammates' strengths and weaknesses.

2. T   F   Don't expect to work on a team where everybody is totally compatible.

3. T   F   Teams and groups are not necessarily the same.

4. T   F   One of the most important points of basic behavior in a group is common courtesy.

5. T   F   One role to avoid in a team is self-confessing.

6.   T   F   According to Stephen Covey, transparency means telling the truth in a way that people can verify.

7.   T   F   A symptom of groupthink is illusion of invulnerability.

8.   T   F   In the forming stage of group development, group cohesiveness begins to emerge.

9.   T   F   Consensus is a perfect agreement of the group.

10. T   F   For groups to be effective, the members must pay attention to both tasks and relationships.

11. T   F   Group task roles help the interpersonal functioning of the group. They strengthen, regulate, and perpetuate the group.

12. T   F   Effective followers share many of the same characteristics as effective leaders.

13. T   F   Ground rules are the behaviors that people in a group consciously or unconsciously agree to use to enable them to work effectively together.

14. T   F   Elaborating is calling attention to oneself through boasting or reporting on personal achievements, acting in inappropriate ways, or fighting.

15. T   F   To work through the storming stage, deal with differences in a timely and open manner.

Answers can be found on page 242.

Meetings

Attending a Meeting

- Arrive early to allow yourself time to find a seat and get situated.
- Be prepared—understand the meeting's topics and related data.

- Use positive and attentive facial expressions.

- Keep your hands on the table where they can be seen. This position looks more professional and signals that you are above-board with nothing to hide.

- Sit as close as possible to the power perch.

- Stand up when you want to make an especially important point.

- Actively listen.

- Silence your electronic devices.

- Stay calm.

- Before asking a question, raise your hand.

> ### Practice Your Speech Before the Meeting
>
> If you know for a fact that you will be called upon to speak in the meeting, rehearse beforehand. Try to appear spontaneous.

- Be brief and stay on topic when you speak.

- If you do arrive late, step in quickly and quietly while taking your seat. Do not make excuses to everyone while the presenter is talking.

- If the meeting is about discussing problems, make sure you have thought out your answers and/or solutions.

- If you must leave early, send notification prior to the meeting and receive confirmation, and take a seat at the beginning of the meeting that will allow you to leave in an unobtrusive manner.

- If you must go to the restroom, be as quiet as possible when you leave and return.

Meeting No-Nos

- Being unprepared (Do whatever it takes for you to be ready if information is shared.)

- Showing up late

- Dominating the meeting

- Sitting silently

- Expressing rude body language (e.g., eye-rolling)
- Conducting sidebar conversations
- Arguing or putting others down
- Leaving your cell phone on
- Cursing or using slang
- Texting during the meeting and/or checking e-mail
- Exhibiting distracting nervous habits (e.g., tapping a pen on a table, making audible noises with your mouth, rustling papers, tapping your feet on the floor, chewing gum)
- Putting your cell phone or any other personal electronic device on the table
- Dressing unprofessionally

Asking Questions at a Meeting

- Hold up your hand to indicate you have a question.
- Never blurt your question out in the middle of the presentation.
- Write down your questions as you think of them, then ask them during the Q&A portion of the meeting.
- Keep your questions simple, direct, and brief.
- Ask only one question at a time and wait for the answer.

Fix a Meeting

You have been told by your supervisor that you will have to lead the weekly meetings in her absence for the next two months. So far, the meetings have been a disaster. What would you do differently? What are some of the general rules you need to follow in order to prepare and be successful?

Chapter 8

Diversity in the Workplace

One day our descendants will think it incredible that we paid so much attention to things like the amount of melanin in our skin or the shape of our eyes or our gender instead of the unique identities of each of us as complex human beings.
—Franklin Thomas

Men hate each other because they fear each other, and they fear each other because they don't know each other, and they don't know each other because they are often separated from each other. —Martin Luther King, Jr.

We all should know that diversity makes for a rich tapestry, and we must understand that all the threads of the tapestry are equal in value no matter what their color. —Maya Angelou

Diversity in the Workplace: What It Is and What It Isn't

Today's workforce does not look, act, or think like the workforce of the past; nor does it hold the same values, have the same experiences, or pursue the same needs and desires. However, when work groups are made up of individuals with many backgrounds, values, cultures, educational levels, physical and mental abilities, and lifestyles, promoting teamwork and productive interactions can be quite a challenge. Since work provides us with the food we eat, the cars we drive, the roof over our heads, and a lot more, it behooves us all to better understand the dynamics of the workplace.

For many, the term *workplace diversity* is a synonym for *affirmative action* or *equal employment opportunity*. Let's examine the differences between these terms.

Equal Employment Opportunity (EEO) = Laws

(Social Concerns)

EEO rulings are **federal laws** designed to combat racism and prejudice in employment practices on the basis of race, gender, age, color, national origin, disability, religion, genetics, and retaliation. Note that recently the U.S. Equal Employment Opportunity Commission equates gender identity discrimination with sex discrimination.

Many state and local governments have expanded their laws to cover criteria such as heritage, sexual orientation, and appearance.

In the federal employment system, discrimination based on sexual orientation, marital status, parental status, political affiliation, and genetic information are prohibited employment practices under Merit System Principles.

Affirmative Action (AA) = Programs

(Social Concerns)

Affirmative action encompasses **programs** designed to overcome the present effects of historical employment discrimination. The focus is on removing barriers to the employment of women, minorities, and people with disabilities. These programs usually exclude White men, but not always.

Affirmative action applies to the government and to private-sector organizations that contract with the federal government or that receive federal financial assistance.

Over the past 60 years, through Supreme Court decisions, it has been made clear that AA programs cannot involve quotas.

Workplace Diversity = Philosophy/Best Practices

(Business Necessity)

Workplace diversity is a **philosophy and/or process** designed to increase productivity and profitability in businesses and organizations. The key concepts are respect and inclusion.

Unlike EEO and AA, it is fueled by economic concerns rather than primarily legal or moral concerns.

It refers to any mixture of items characterized by differences and similarities within an organization.

Diversity focuses on the collective mixture (people, concepts, concrete items, or abstractions), not just pieces of it.

The philosophy of diversity is to support innovation, creativity, and individuality as the means for achieving the organization's mission goals and realizing business success.

Some equate workplace diversity with only race and gender, but diversity is a much larger concept. *Diversity* in the workplace is an **umbrella term** that encompasses the **similarities, differences,** and **tensions** of such employees as:

- White men
- Gay, lesbian, bisexual, and transgender people
- Disabled individuals
- Functionally illiterate persons
- Baby boomers
- Parent caregivers
- Immigrants to the United States
- Single parents

Diversity can also refer to social, cultural, functional, and historical dimensions such as:

- Physical/mental ability
- Values and perceptions
- Organizational functions
- Geographical location
- Sexual orientation
- Processing of information
- Religious beliefs and practices
- Military/veteran status
- Language facility

- Socioeconomic level
- Immigrant status
- Work styles or functions
- Race
- Lifestyles
- Gender
- Ethnicity
- Age
- Family makeup

Workplace diversity encompasses the diversity of clients, customers, employees, contractors, and suppliers.

The Platinum Rule

Pt Platinum

Atomic Number: 78
Atomic Mass: 195.02

Treat others as they want to be treated.

The Platinum Rule is an expansion of the Golden Rule. We cannot assume that others want to be treated exactly the same way we do.

Diversity Life Experiences Assessment

How diverse has your life been so far? What were the messages sent to you about people who were different from you?

On a scale of 1 (*low; no daily interaction*) to 5 (*high; daily interaction*), rate the level of diversity you have experienced in the following organizations and groups with which you are or have been affiliated. For purposes of this exercise, *diversity* is defined as differences in race, ethnicity, gender, age, religion, disability, sexual orientation, or socioeconomic level.

Put a check (✓) in the appropriate column and answer the questions that follow.

Organization or group	1	2	3	4	5
Home / family					
Community / neighborhood where you grew up					
Nursery school / elementary school					
Middle school / junior high / high school					
Military					
College / university					
Sorority / fraternity					
Girl Scouts, Boy Scouts, other civic organizations					
Church, temple, synagogue					
Professional association					
Social organization					
Former work organization					
Current work organization					
Community / neighborhood where you now live					
Any additional organizations / affiliations (specify)					

Discussion Questions

1. How diverse has your life been so far? When did your diversity experiences begin?

2. What were the reasons for the diversity or lack of diversity experiences in your life?

3. What implicit or explicit messages were you given as a child about people who were different from you?

4. How have your experiences prepared you for working in a diverse workforce?

Dimensions of Diversity

Note. Adapted from Loden & Rosener (1990).

Dimensions describe the properties and characteristics that constitute the whole person. Every individual enters the workplace with a unique perspective shaped by these dimensions and past experiences.

Primary (internal) dimensions are considered those immutable human differences that an individual is born with and/or that exert an important impact on our early socialization and an ongoing impact throughout our lives. These six primary dimensions serve as interdependent core elements. Our life experiences are filtered through them. What we see and experience throughout our lives cannot be separated from these primary dimensions because our thoughts, feelings, and behaviors are inextricably linked to them.

Primary dimensions are aspects of ourselves that we cannot change. They are things people note about us before we even open our mouths. When people feel they are being stereotyped based on a primary dimension, they can be very sensitive. The six primary dimensions are:

age	ethnicity	physical/mental qualities
race	sexual orientation	gender

Secondary (external) dimensions are mutable differences that we acquire, discard, and/or modify throughout our lives. Theses dimensions add contour and breath to our self-definition. In some instances, one or several of these secondary dimensions can exert an impact as powerful as those of the primary dimensions. Secondary dimensions are aspects of ourselves that we have some power to change. We also have a choice of whether to disclose this information or not; we can conceal it. The secondary dimensions of diversity include but are not limited to:

educational background	geographic location
income	marital status
military experience	parental status
religious beliefs	work experience

Organizational dimensions are aspects of us within the workplace. These dimensions exert an impact as powerful as primary or secondary dimensions. Organizational dimensions include but are not limited to:

functional level	classification
work location	union affiliation
geographic location	seniority
work content/field	division/department
management status	

Dimensions of Diversity

1. What are the most identifiable and pertinent diversity dimensions in your life?

2. What diversity challenges did you or do you face? How do they show up in the workplace?

3. How do you handle the diversity challenges?

4. How have you been successful?

Valuing Diversity

Valuing diversity does not mean you will like all people who are different from you. But it does mean showing respect and inclusion in the workplace. Valuing diversity is a philosophy based on tenets such as:

- Diversity within the workplace environment adds value to the environment and creates a strength based culture.

- People are more the same than they are different.

- Differences add value to organizations and groups.

- People are created equally and are deserving of equal, impartial treatment.

- It is economically important for the organization to have and manage diversity.

- There is a broad range of group identities and they can all have an effect on employment.

On a personal level, valuing diversity means:

- **Examining** your individual comfort levels;

- **Creating** opportunities to enhance your awareness, understanding, and acceptance of differences among people;

- **Accepting** and not denying differences in the human race;

- **Avoiding** prejudging people;

- **Learning** to appreciate individuality; and

- **Respecting** yourself and others.

Suggestions for Valuing Diversity

- Pay attention and really listen to others—what they say and the feelings they express.

- Separate the people from the problem.

- Don't make assumptions about how others think, feel, or might react. You cannot get into anyone's head. Crystal-ball-gazing is for fortune tellers.

- Sarcasm and kidding are considered dirty fighting.

- Don't be constructively generous. Let others exercise their rights to be responsible for themselves.

- Try to send harmonious messages to avoid confusing people.

- Disagree with or confront unrealistic or manipulative behavior, but don't attack others as people.

- Don't play manipulative games. Be honest, direct, open, and specific.

- Don't correct others' statements about how they feel, and don't tell them how they should feel.

- Don't label people as dumb, cowardly, lazy, or childish, and don't make sweeping judgments about feelings—especially about whether the feeling is real or important, or morally right or wrong.

- Be careful about how you use questions. They can be a demanding, controlling form of communication, especially the "why" or "why not" questions, which can imply disapproval.

- Don't state your opinions as facts, avoid preaching words (e.g., "you *should* . . ."), and don't exaggerate or bulldoze others.

- When you have differences, be willing to mediate. And when you do fight, fight fair.

Are You Diversity-Challenged?

Dr. R. Roosevelt Thomas (2006) defines the *diversity-challenged* as people who acknowledge having difficulty making quality decisions in the midst of differences, similarities, and tensions.

A diversity-mature person:

- Identifies any discomforts with the dynamics of diversity

- Acknowledges being diversity-challenged

- Recognizes the cost of being diversity-challenged

- Accepts personal diversity management responsibility

- Challenges conventional wisdom

- Engages in continuous learning

To be effective in a diverse organization, employees need to be:

- **Aware** of their own values and know how comfortable they are with diversity and their own and others' biases.

- **Accepting** of their own limitations and those of others, as well as their own mistakes.

- **Able** to accept the premise that *different* is not *inferior*.

- **Committed** to constant learning—knowing it is virtually impossible to learn everything one needs to know about diversity.

- **Flexible** in unanticipated situations and willing to modify their own behavior and the system.

- **Willing** to live by the "Platinum Rule."

Questions to Address:

1. What aspects of diversity are you most uncomfortable interacting with or talking about at work?

2. What aspects of diversity are subtly or obviously contentious at work? For example: Facing special challenges, overhearing bigoted or stereotyping statements, or witnessing prejudicial behaviors.

3. What steps can you take as an individual to overcome your discomfort?

Sources of Diversity Tensions

While discrimination in the workplace is still prevalent, the majority of employees in the workplace do not intentionally go to work to disrespect and discriminate against those who are different from them. Many forms of discrimination occur without the offender's knowledge.

Micro-Inequities

Small Slights Can Lead to Huge Problems.

A major source of tension in the workplace is micro-inequities. Micro-inequities are small communications of disrespect and inequity—like small paper cuts. Paper cuts hurt!

Micro-inequities cannot be eliminated by legal mandates under EEO in the workplace. They usually exist beneath the radar of unlawful behavior. Micro-inequities are small messages of bias that are sent from one person to another, often without knowing. No one is immune from micro-inequities.

Micro-inequities are small events which are often ephemeral (short-lived) and hard-to-prove, events which are covert, often unintentional, frequently unrecognized by the perpetrator, and occur whenever people are perceived to be "different."

- The likelihood of encountering micro-inequities increases the more that someone is perceived to be different.

- Micro-inequities work both by excluding the different person and by making that person less self-confident and less productive

- Subtle messages, sometime unconscious that devalues, discourage and ultimately impairs performance in the workplace

- Work both by excluding the different person and by making that person less self-confident and less productive.

- No one is immune from micro-inequities. It is estimated that we send thousands of micro-messages every day.

- Micro-inequities cannot be eliminated by legal mandates.

- According to research, micro-inequities cost U.S. employers $64 billion per year (the cost of losing and replacing employees who quit their jobs solely due to workplace unfairness).

Examples of micro-inequities:

- Ignoring cultural needs, differences, or sensitivities

- Interrupting someone while he or she is speaking

- Failing to acknowledge someone's presence

- Excluding someone from relevant e-mail

- Neglecting someone during introductions

- Never bothering to learn the correct pronunciation of a person's name

- Rolling eyes or sighing when someone considered "different" is speaking

- Manager not acknowledging coworkers or subordinates

- Not paying attention in meetings when a certain person is sharing an idea

- Suggestions put forth by a member of the out-group (someone "different") being ignored, but being favorably received when suggested by a member of the in-group (or "dominant" group)

- Exclusion of environmental factors that represent a certain group (e.g., decorations, literature, artwork)

- Absence of informal mentoring

The only way to deal with micro-inequities is to bring them to the forefront through discussion.

Micro-affirmations (Valuing Behavior)

Micro-affirmations are ephemeral, hard-to-see events that are public and private, often unconscious but very effective. They occur wherever people wish to help others succeed.

Although micro-affirmations are only tiny gestures of inclusion, respect, caring, and listening, they make people feel valued and acknowledged. Because they boost morale and create feelings of inclusion, micro-affirmations are excellent at counteracting micro-inequities:

- If a person affirms another, they are blocking possibilities of creating inequities. Therefore, micro-affirmations block unwanted, negative behavior (micro-inequities). The two cannot happen simultaneously.

- The snowballing nature of affirming and appreciating an individual has the potential to reverse the effects created by inequities.

- Micro-affirmations have a built-in role model effect: Witnessing small, appreciative acts allows others to see its effects and invites them to replicate them, influencing their behavior and possibly their environment.

Examples of micro-affirmations:

- Saying "hello" and "goodbye"

- Giving a nod or a smile

- Making eye contact

- Inviting someone to join the group during lunch time

- Having the audience pay full attention to an individual's presentation without texting

- Not interrupting someone while he or she is speaking

- Saying "please" and "thank you"

Stereotypes

> *"Stereotypes are fixed and distorted generalizations made about all members of a particular group; rigid judgments which do not take into account the here and now."*

—Marilyn Loden

Stereotypes:

- Are overgeneralizations that tell us what to expect of those who are different;

- Are learned from family, childhood, peers, and media;

- Can be positive or negative;

- Can cause us to ignore, avoid, or act aggressively toward others; and

- Can distort our vision in a minor or extreme manner.

We can all stereotype. Despite how hard we try to remain objective, everyone develops some prejudices and stereotypes about others because of early socialization. Beyond our socialization, we stereotype as a selective device to simplify perception and thinking.

However, by negating people's individuality and value, stereotypes have a destructive, dysfunctional impact. In most situations, they minimize the talents, potential, and accomplishments of others.

Stereotypes frequently reinforce an underlying prejudice about others that stems from a superiority/inferiority belief system. When someone does not fit into a negative stereotype, we create a subcategory—an "exception to the rule."

It takes serious mental effort to give up negative stereotypes, no matter how many "exceptions" we encounter.

Collusion

> *"Cooperation with others, knowingly or unknowingly, to reinforce stereotypical attitudes, prevailing behaviors, and norms."*

—Marilyn Loden

Types of collusion include: silence, denial, and active cooperation.

Self-Fulfilling Prophecies

A self-fulfilling prophecy is the tendency of our expectations to foster the behavior that is consistent with our expectations. Any positive or negative expectation about circumstances, events, or people that may affect a person's behavior toward them in a manner that causes those expectations to be fulfilled can be called a self-fulfilling prophecy. This is also known as the Pygmalion Effect.

Robert Rosenthal and Lenore Jacobson, in 1968, gave all the children in an elementary class a test and told teachers that some of children were unusually clever (though they were actually average). They came back at the end of the school year and tested the same class again. Guess what? The children singled out as "clever" had improved their scores far more than other children. This phenomenon applies to the workplace as well.

- If a person thinks we are stupid, he or she will treat us that way. If we are treated as if we are stupid, we will likely act—and therefore become—this way. The person has thus had a prophecy about us fulfilled!

- A supervisor who thinks that an employee is more intelligent than other employees may praise the employee to a greater degree than other employees. As a result, the employee achieves greater job performance than the other employees.

Often, people act as we expect them to when expectations come from negative stereotypes.

Beyond the personal anguish and interpersonal conflict that stereotyping causes when it occurs, there is a more damaging long-term impact. Left unchecked, stereotyping can play a major role in lowering creativity, productivity, and employee morale. It can even become a predictor of behavior. By continuously reacting to and reinforcing particular responses in others, we can increase the likelihood that these behaviors prevail. **If we see people as competent and treat them accordingly, they will act competently.**

Passive Bias

Passive bias is a term coined by Lawrence Otis Graham in his 1997 book, *Proversity.* It is bigoted behavior that seems benign and that is not intended to harm or insult others. You may be exhibiting passive bias in the following situations:

- What you notice first about people around you are the characteristics that make them different from you.

- When others make bigoted remarks or jokes, you either laugh or say nothing because you don't want to seem sensitive or self-righteous.

- When you look for a mentor or a protégé, you pick someone who reminds you of yourself.

- You are affiliated with an organization like a country club, women's club, lodge, etc., that practices subtle discrimination, but you say nothing because you didn't create the group's rules.

- Before you hire someone for a position, you have a vague picture in your mind of what the ideal candidate would probably look like.

- Your conversations often make use of phrases like "you people," "our kind," or "those people."

Hidden Biases

Managers' subtle biases and acts of discrimination are often the reasons why employees file employment complaints, detach emotionally from their work, leave organizations, or sue. Generally, managers in the dominant culture will assume members of their own culture are competent, but will require members of outside groups to prove their competency.

Hidden biases manifest themselves as human-resource issues related to employee credibility, exclusionary practices, and double standards. Collectively these biases, which are rooted in general stereotypes of those outside of the dominant culture group, impact the ability of women, people of color, and others to advance. This puts them at a distinct disadvantage, as evidenced by the following examples.

- A White manager tells an African American coworker, "You are so articulate!"

- A woman makes a suggestion at a meeting, but none of the men acknowledge it or respond. Five minutes later, a man makes the same suggestion. He is applauded and praised.

- An Asian American colleague is asked by an African American coworker, "Where are you from?" The colleague responds "Cleveland." The coworker then asks, "No, I mean, what country are you from?"

- A White female engineer who is double-checking calculations in a set of plans calls her Latina colleague and asks, "Are you certain this is correct?" She then calls another White colleague to check the Latina colleague's calculations. She never questions his calculations.

- A planning committee is discussing an off-site training session. The team leader says, "Not all of us have to go if the building isn't accessible."

- A disabled employee writes a well-written report and her abled supervisor asks, "Did you write this by yourself?"

Attitudinal Barriers

Attitudinal barriers are ways of thinking or feeling resulting in behavior that limit the potential of disabled people to be independent individuals. They include dehumanizing, generalizing, disempowering, using oppressive language, segregating, overprotecting, and excluding.

Dehumanizing

- Seeing the person only in terms of the disability

- Not recognizing the whole person; assuming everything in a person's life—emotions, relationships, work, choices—revolves around his or her disability

- Acting as if people with disabilities have no emotions, no sexuality, impaired intelligence, and/or are unable to make decisions for themselves
- Hiring people with disabilities only for easy tasks at low pay; assuming that people with disabilities do not need to earn a self-supporting wage
- Not talking directly to the disabled person
- Not establishing eye contact with, or staring at, the disabled person

Generalizing

- Denying disabled people's uniqueness as individuals
- Assuming that one disabled person represents all people with disabilities
- Assuming that someone with one disability necessarily has others, too (e.g., believing that someone with a speech impediment must also have an intellectual disability)
- Not recognizing the diversity of disabilities or the diversity of people who share any particular disability
- Searching for the single right answer about how to act around people with disabilities; not recognizing that every individual is in a different place with his or her own process and self-identity

Disempowering

- Assuming that people with disabilities cannot know what is best for themselves
- Not listening to people with disabilities
- Imposing "help" rather than offering it, and thereby taking control away from the person
- Withholding the authority and/or information that would enable a person with a disability to make his or her own decisions
- Always hiring able-bodied people to design and administer social services for people with disabilities

Using Oppressive Language

- Equating *sick* with *bad*, as in "ill-will," "ill-fated," "sickening" (i.e., "disgusting")

Segregating

- Hiring people with disabilities only to work in handicapped services
- Believing people with disabilities will all want work related to their disability
- Assuming people with disabilities should work or learn only with other people with disabilities
- Scheduling only special activities for accessibility, rather than making all activities accessible

Overprotecting

- Holding lower expectations of people with disabilities, or giving work that's too easy; for example, celebrating minor accomplishments as miraculous (obviously a minor accomplishment for one person may be a major one for another—the point is to react appropriately to the specific case)
- Soft-pedaling negative feedback for fear of a disabled person's reaction
- Making decisions for people with disabilities to shelter them from failing or getting hurt
- Tracking people with disabilities into only certain job fields

Excluding

- Not shaking hands
- Not including a disabled person in social or work-related activities
- Choosing activities or meeting places that are inaccessible (no elevators or wide bathrooms for people with wheelchairs, no sign language translators, etc.)
- Seeking a disabled person's opinion or perspective only on issues related to disability; imagining that he or she does not have valuable opinions and experience on the same breadth of issues you do

Moving Beyond the Tensions

The **bias virus** is remarkably resistant. One reason for this toughness is that most of us just can't stand being wrong and will do almost anything to prove our bias correct. Our biases are attitudes, not behaviors; but we act based on our attitudes. Our biases can provide us with the desired illusion that we can predict the behavior and characteristics of people who are different from ourselves.

Psychologists call this process *belief perseverance* and have identified numerous mind games we play to keep our biases alive. For example, we:

- Ignore or forget information that does not support our bias

- Distort any contradictory evidence that comes—"You are the exception"

- Give extra weight and credence to information that validates our bias

- Rationalize and distort what we see to make it conform to our bias

- Act on our bias in a way that allows it to become a self-fulfilling prophecy

So . . .

- **Self-reflect.** Acknowledge and accept responsibility for your biases, stereotypes, blind spots, and personal prejudices.

- **Identify** the way(s) it operates in your life (your behavior).

- **Assess** the impact of your behavior on others and yourself at work.

- **Modify** negative behavior by using

  - **Consideration**—Listening, empathizing, and following the "platinum rule."

  - **Respect**—Showing regard for all differences and valuing the talents each person brings to the workplace.

  - **Learning**—Being open and receptive to information about the different cultures, customs, and perspectives of others. Communicate with kindness and clarity.

- **Obtain feedback** by stepping out of your comfort zone and associating with those who are *different* from you.

- **Recognize and question** stereotypical thinking in yourself and others.

- **Get to know people** as individuals.

Steps to reduce diversity tensions and its effects include:

- Listening

- Formal education and training

- Seeking and checking information from members of other identity groups in order to distinguish real intergroup difference from folklore and myths

- Requesting feedback from people about the group's use of stereotypes

- Challenging other people about their assumptions and statements when they appear to be based on stereotypes

- Following the "platinum rule"

- Being open and receptive to information about the different cultures, customs and perspectives of others

- Communicating with kindness and clarity

Generations in the Workplace

A *generation* is an entire body of individuals born and living about the same time. Aside from the coincidence of birth, these individuals share common experiences, attitudes, and tastes. The four generations of today's workplace cover over 60 birth years, from about 1934 to 2000. These four generations are clearly distinguishable by all their demographics; their early life experiences; the headlines that defined their times; their heroes, music, and sociology; and their early days in the workplace. Look at the four generations and think about the impacts of their collective events.

Generational Issues

- Different work ethic
- Long hours vs. free time as a priority
- 9–5 vs. flexibility
- Approach to work
- Communication modes
- The use of technology
- Seniority versus performance-based structures
- Work–life balance
- Flexible work options
- Time off
- Educational and personal growth

Tips for Working With Any Generation

Do . . .

- Recognize that generational differences influence our ideas, expectations, values, and behaviors at work.
- Acknowledge that everyone wants to be treated with respect—and recognize that respect might look and feel different based on differing experiences and perspectives.
- Know that you have different life experiences and can learn from others' experiences and perspectives.
- Find ways to create shared values and common ground.
- Be willing to alter your natural style and preferences in order to work effectively with all your colleagues.
- Be open and honest about your "hot buttons" (recurring sources of tension or conflict).

Four Generations in the Workplace

Radio Babies | The Silent Generation | Traditionals

Born 1922–1944

Baby Boomers | TV Babies

Born 1945–1961

Generation X | Computer Babies

Born 1962–1980

Millennials | Generation Y

Born 1981–2002

Cuspers

- People born near the end of one generation or the beginning of the next generation (3- to 5-year span)
- Often share the characteristics of two generations and can relate well to both

- Give your colleagues specific suggestions on what they can do to help you perform your best.

- Focus on what really matters: productivity, teamwork, and customer relationships.

- Challenge assumptions and raise awareness regarding the multi-generational workplace.

Don't . . .

- Stereotype—e.g., judging your colleague's capabilities by what they wear and what his or her work hours seem to be.

- Ridicule or call derogatory names like "dinosaur," "bureaucrat," "slacker," or "kid."

- Miss opportunities to improve communications and strengthen relationships.

- **Finally, don't assume every member of any given generation thinks or behaves exactly alike.**

Talkin' 'Bout Our Generations

1. What does your generation bring to a work team?

2. What would you prefer people did not say about your generation?

3. What would you want people to know about your generation to improve relationships in the workplace?

4. What do all generations in the workplace have in common?

Dr. Martin Luther King's Model

People hate each other because they fear each other; they fear each other because they don't know each other; they don't know each other because they are often separated from each other.

If you reverse this:

Associate more ⇨ Know more ⇨ Communicate more ⇨ Understand more ⇨ Fear less

Trust

(Originally developed by Alexander Consulting and Training)

Trust in the *Webster's Dictionary* is defined as reliance on the integrity, strength, ability, surety, etc., of a person. Trust is very important in a diverse workplace. The level of trust among team members affects how ideas are generated, how decisions are made, and how conflicts are resolved.

Fear	No Trust	Confidence
Distrust	No Distrust	Trust

- Think of trust as a sliding scale. At one end of the scale you distrust and at the other end you trust.

- Almost all relations begin in the middle with no trust or distrust. Through tests in incremental steps, we move either toward trust or toward distrust.

- Many of us tend to stay in the middle, with no trust and no distrust. However, you cannot improve a relationship until positive trust has been established. Remember: Zero multiplied by any number is still zero.

In addition to the presence or absence of trust, it is also important to consider the *level* of trust between people.

Level 1: Respectful Regard

"I believe you mean me no deliberate harm."

Level 2: Committed Consistency

"I believe you will consider my interests even when I am not present."

Level 3: Active Awareness

"I believe you understand me and act in my best interests."

Trust-Building Tips

- Be consistent in your behavior with others.

- Use self-disclosure. Share who you are as a person. Show your humanness.

- Admit challenges and mistakes. Apologize.

- Tell the truth. Be as honest and open as you can, or explain why you cannot tell everything.

- Give and receive constructive feedback without malice.

- Share information with others. Be open regarding issues that do not require confidentiality.

- Keep confidences about sensitive matters.

- Keep your word. Always follow through on promises and commitments. Meet deadlines, respond, and call or deliver when you say you will.

- Be a problem solver. Look for win-win solutions to problems.

- Perform above the norm. Go beyond what is expected of you.

Race in the Workplace

Instead of looking at race, which really does not exist, look at the model of the **cultural context inventory**, which is based on behaviors.

Based on the work of anthropologist Edward Hall as described in Halverson (1993), cultures can be placed on a continuum from high to low context. The term *context* refers to the interrelated conditions in which something exists—social and cultural conditions that influence the life of an individual, organization, or community.

Where do you fall on Hall's continuum?

	Low Context	*High Context*
Association	• Relationships begin and end quickly.	• Relationships depend on trust, build up slowly, and are stable.
	• Things get done by following procedures.	• Things get done based on relationships with people.
	• One's identity is rooted in oneself and accomplishments.	• One's identity is rooted in groups.
	• Social structure is decentralized; responsibility goes further down.	• Social structure and authority are centralized; responsibility is at top.
Interaction	• Low use of nonverbal elements.	• High use of nonverbal elements.
	• Verbal message is explicit; context is less important than words.	• Verbal message is implicit; context is more important than words.
	• Verbal message is direct.	• Verbal message is indirect.
	• Disagreement is depersonalized.	• Disagreement is personalized.
Territorality	• Privacy is important, so people are farther apart.	• Space is communal: People stand close to each other, share the same space.
Temporality	• Things are scheduled to be done at particular times, one thing at a time.	• Time is not easily scheduled; needs of people may interfere with keeping to a set time.
	• Change is fast.	• Change is slow.
	• Time is a commodity to be spent or saved.	• Time is a process; it belongs to others and to nature.
	• Speed is valued.	
Learning	• Learning occurs by following directions and explanations.	• Learning occurs by first observing others and then practicing.
	• Individuals are preferred for learning and problem solving.	• Groups are preferred for learning and problem solving.
		• Accuracy is valued.

	Low Context	*High Context*
Areas/ groups	• Scandinavia • Germany • United States Whites (Medium-Low) • Urban	• Latin America • Hispanic Americans • Asia • Asian Americans • Africa • African Americans • Rural

The Meaning of Race in Science

The following statements are based on testimony given at the President's Cancer Panel Meeting of April 9, 1997 (Freeman, 1998):

- Races (genetically homogeneous populations) do not exist in the human species today, nor is there any evidence that they have ever existed.

- "The biologic concept of race is untenable and has no legitimate place in biologic science."

- Studies reveal that approximately 85% of all variation in gene frequencies occurs within populations or races and only 15% occurs between such populations.

- Racial and ethnic categories used in the census are constructs which have no basis in science or anthropology.

- Racism is part of societal, institutional, and civilizational values that have influenced scientific thought.

Interacting With People Outside the United States

Don't assume that employees from other countries will accept your American mannerisms as cute or novel. In fact, some of your mannerisms may be offensive.

Remember we in the United States tend to be very direct. Generally we are pretty up-front; when we speak, we usually get right to the point. Usually there are no double meanings, no hidden agendas, and no subtle hints. However, some people from other countries think we are rude because of our straightforward way of speaking.

Many cultures closely observe volume, vocal quality, tone of voice, and posture because they indicate good breeding. Therefore, don't speak loudly or monopolize conversations; listen more than you speak.

We demand promptness in time. Our focus is to use time efficiently to get the maximum out of every minute. That is not the way many other people in the world think about time. Every culture has different expectations about scheduling and appointments. For many cultures, time is flexible. If you are brusque, rushing around and cutting to the chase, you might not be successful in dealings with people from other cultures. Always try to be flexible.

Following are some tips to avoid faux pas (blunders, indiscretions, mistakes):

On Gesturing

- In many parts of the world, a thumbs-up is an obscene gesture.

- People outside the United States, especially people from Asian countries, consider pointing the index finger rude.

- The American "bye-bye" gesture means "come here" to people from Southeast Asia.

- In Brazil and Portugal, the "okay" gesture that you make with your index finger and thumb is considered obscene.

- In Germany, people start counting on their fingers with the thumb, not the index finger. So if you hold up your index finger to indicate that you want one item, you may end up with two.

On Conversing

- Don't ask personal questions.

- Don't criticize the person's country or city.

- Don't compare the person's country to the United States.

- Don't mistakenly denigrate the country or city you're visiting by saying that it's cute, quaint, or old-fashioned.

- Don't discuss politics, local royalty, religion, or customs.

- Don't tell jokes (they often don't translate well).

- Don't say anything in English that you wouldn't want to be overheard if you said it in the local language.

- But do pay compliments on the culture, beauty, and achievements of the country or city you are visiting.

On Dressing

- Dress conservatively, conventionally, and appropriately. Less flash is better.

- Show less of your skin; remember the four *B*s!

When you receive someone's business card, do not put it away immediately in your pocket or purse; doing so may indicate disrespect. Keep the card in front of you at the conference table and refer to it throughout the meeting.

Managing Your Multicultural Starship

In 1966 the Starship Enterprise set out on its five-year mission with an unusual crew on the bridge: a crew that represented every color and creed in the human spectrum, and one race not even from Earth. It was a minor miracle for a television network to show a Black woman and an Asian man in positions of managerial responsibility. Now, more than 35 years later, it has become a commonplace. Corporate reality. No one notices the "miracle" of interracial presence in the Star Trek reruns anymore. No one notices the even more miraculous management achievements of Captain Kirk. He is a multicultural manager and—at least on television—a very successful one.

Let's take a look at the Enterprise crew. Dr. McCoy, from the U.S. state of Georgia, has the prickly personal honor of a "Southern gentleman" and is quick to react with outrage at anything he sees an as affront to his sense of dignity. Lt. Uhura—whose name is the Swahili word for freedom—grew up in Africa. Lt. Commander Scott ("Scotty") may have a Scottish brogue, but he is the true spiritual brother of every competent blue-collar worker who ever came up through the ranks to management. Ensign Chekhov is a Russian Chauvinist who seldom misses a chance to explain how Russians invented the airplane, radio, and impulse engine. Ensign Sulu's family tree includes people from many parts of the Orient and, as such, he is heir to the oldest human cultural tradition. And Mr. Spock is . . . well, Mr. Spock is Mr. Spock—someone whose cultural background is ultimately unknowable.

First, Captain Kirk is clear about his mission and he makes sure that it is clear to everyone who works with him. He is also clear that "seeking out new worlds" has nothing to do with what language his crew members learned at birth, how long their hair is, or how they decorate their cabins. Kirk does not allow himself or anyone else to act as if the goal of the Enterprise is to have everyone conform to a stereotype.

Next, Captain Kirk pays attention to the differences among his crew members and he respects them. When Mr. Spock states that the probability is "point nine three" that evacuating the colonists from Rigel 9 will fatally infect members of the Enterprise crew with their plague, Kirk does not tell Mr. Spock that he is an inhuman calculating machine. When Dr. McCoy says: "You can't just leave them down there to die, Jim. Let me get some of the colonists into sick bay, so I can try to find an anti-toxin," Kirk does not tell McCoy that he is a bleeding heart who is completely ignoring the danger to the Enterprise. Captain Kirk—the multi-cultural manager—is aware of the personality and cultural background of his subordinates. Spock and McCoy have both made important points. If Kirk insists that his crew conform to a single cultural style in all their expression, he will not only alienate a substantial portion of his crew, but—much worse—he may never hear anything at all from many of his subordinates.

Captain Kirk also insists that the members of his crew respect each other. It is never acceptable for one crew member to insult another. Russian, Georgian, Black, female, or Vulcan . . . any crew member who attacks another on that basis is wrong. It is the act of making the attack that is important. Kirk knows that he cannot change the personal prejudices of his crew, but he can and does insist that those prejudices are not expressed in any work context. No doubt Captain Kirk does not accept new crew members who cannot communicate around their cultural bias.

Captain Kirk knows that he has blind spots. I am sure that Kirk spends some of his off-duty hours on "continuing education for Starship Captains." No doubt this includes studying the different ways that people in the Federation think and behave. Kirk knows that the attitudes of his crew will surprise him from time to time. When it happens, he makes an extra effort to discover the crew member's point of view before he assumes that the crew member is behaving irrationally or committing a breach of discipline.

There is really nothing about the management style of Captain James T. Kirk that is unknown to enlightened managers of the twenty-first century. Kirk focuses on organizational goals, listens and communicates well, and enforces mutual respect among his subordinates. Nonetheless, Captain Kirk benefits from a multicultural perspective. We all know that if we want to manage from a multicultural perspective, we must:

- Recognize that differences (cultural, gender, sexual orientation, age, etc.) do exist.

- Learn about other cultures.

- Learn about our own cultural background, style, and conditioning.

- Respect and be sensitive to individual differences and cultures.

- Root-out stereotypes.

- Set and communicate the goals for our organization.

- Explain the rules for workplace behavior.

- Hold people accountable after explaining the rules.

- Demand that workers respect one another on the job.
- Aspire to flexibility.

We can only guess what the Starfleet Academy taught Captain Kirk about managing a multicultural workforce, but I believe that we are going to have to learn those lessons much sooner than most people think. Managers with a monocultural perspective will not be employable in the twenty-first century.

They certainly will never command a Starship.

Managing Your Multicultural Starship

The above article identifies effective traits for valuing and celebrating diversity. In the space below, identify your current level of performance in each using the following scale:

1 = *not currently doing anything*

2 = *performing in a poor to mediocre manner*

3 = *performing on an average level*

4 = *performing in an above average manner*

5 = *doing an outstanding job*

After completing your ratings, identify your strengths in each area and describe a strategy or strategies for increasing your strengths and developmental needs or weaknesses.

1. I examine my comfort levels with those who are different, and I know my blind spots as they relate to valuing diversity.

1   2   3   4   5

Strengths	Weaknesses	Strategies

2. I create opportunities to enhance my awareness, understanding, and acceptance of differences among people.

1   2   3   4   5

Strengths	Weaknesses	Strategies

3. I avoid prejudging people who are different from me when I initially meet them.

1   2   3   4   5

Strengths	Weaknesses	Strategies

Strengths	Weaknesses	Strategies

4. I pay attention to individual differences.

1   2   3   4   5

Strengths	Weaknesses	Strategies

5. I show respect for individual differences.

1   2   3   4   5

Strengths	Weaknesses	Strategies

On a Final Note: Celebrating Diversity

To celebrate diversity means to not just to tolerate differences, but value them. It means we are glad diversity exists. It means we would rather be exposed to the things that make others different from us—their behavior, thinking, choices, and styles.

The challenge is letting go of our present views, opening up to new ones, and being flexible.

Chapter 9
Assertive Communication

📄 *Note: Reading this chapter on assertive communication will not instantly make you assertive. This is not a step-by-step program, but reading the chapter and completing the exercise can start you on the road to communicating more assertively.*

Assertiveness is the ability to:

- express your feelings;

- choose how you will behave, especially in stressful situations;

- speak up for your rights when it is appropriate;

- enhance your self-esteem;

- help yourself develop self-confidence;

- disagree when you think it is important;

- carry out plans for modifying your own behavior; and

- ask others to change their offensive behavior.

No one is born assertive. People tend to place several obstacles between themselves and the goal of assertiveness, including:

- their negative image of themselves,

- their learned fear of conflict situations, and

- their poor communication skills.

Assertiveness is an attitude (style of thinking) associated with specific behaviors. It is a choice of behaviors. It is a set of skills you must practice on a daily basis in order to develop. While passive or aggressive behaviors may be more appropriate responses in some situations, overall, assertiveness is a preferred communication style.

To become assertive, you must have a positive self-concept and believe you can act effectively.

Freeze—Flight—Fight

Assertiveness can be associated with the *fight-or-flight* response, our body's primitive, automatic, tacit response that prepares the body to flee or fight from any perceived attack, harm, or threat to our survival. When we experience excessive stress—whether from internal worry or external circumstance—a bodily reaction is triggered, called the "fight or flight" response. Originally discovered by the Harvard physiologist Walter Cannon, this response is hard-wired into our brains and represents a genetic wisdom designed to protect us from bodily harm. This response actually corresponds to an area of our brain called the hypothalamus, which when stimulated prepares our body for running or fighting.

However, even before the flight sequence there is the "freeze response" or "freezing," typically referred to as hyper-vigilance (being on guard, watchful, or hyper-alert). This initial freeze response is the "stop, look, and listen" response associated with fear. After this initial freeze response, the next response in the sequence is an attempt to flee, and once this has been exhausted, there is an attempt to fight. But suppose the fight-or-flight response is not necessary . . .

One way to understand assertion is to see it as a constructive way of defending one's space and impacting other people. A useful and more common way of defining *assertion* is to place it on a continuum (sliding scale) between flight (submissive behavior) and fight (aggressive behavior). Assertiveness strikes a balance between two known extremes: aggressiveness and submissiveness.

Flight (Fear) Submissive behavior	Assertive behavior	**Fight (Anger)** Aggressive behavior
←		→
(I lose, you win)	(I win, you win)	(I win, you lose)

No one is consistently assertive. All of us use the following three behaviors styles described, depending on the situation and personal factors. Note that people, particularly in situations of disagreement, potential conflict, frustration, or anger exhibit all the above behavior responses.

Assertive Philosophy

Assertive behavior easily becomes habitual when your core beliefs and values are based on an assertive philosophy. The philosophy of assertion is based on the premise that all individuals possess certain rights, including:

1. The right to refuse requests without feeling guilty or selfish

2. The right to have one's own needs considered as important as the needs of others

3. The right to say *no* to requests or demands which cannot be met

4. The right to express oneself as long as the rights of others are not violated

5. The right to your feelings (others may disagree with your opinion, but they cannot disagree with your feelings)

6. The right to ask for what you want

7. The right to be treated with dignity and respect

8. The right to have ones needs and wants respected by others

9. The right to change and grow

10. The right to be listened to

11. The right to be in a non-abusive environment

12. The right to define what respect means to you

13. The right to disagree

14. The right to make mistakes and be responsible for them

15. The right to have your ideas heard

16. The right to judge your own behavior, thoughts, and emotional intelligence and to take the responsibility for their consequences upon yourself.

Body Language Signals

	Submissive	Assertive	Aggressive
Posture	• slumped • shoulders forward • shifting often • chin down • legs entwined while sitting	• erect but relaxed • shoulders straight • few shifts, comfortable stance • head straight • legs together or crossed while sitting • leaning forward	• erect but tense, rigid • shoulders back • jerky shifts or plated in place • chin up or thrusted forward • heels on desk, hands behind head while sitting or tensely leaning forward
Gestures	• fluttered hands • twisted motions • shoulders shrugs • frequent head nodding	• casual head movements • relaxed hands • hands open, palms out • occasional head nodding	• chopping or jabbing with hands • clenched hands or pointing • sweeping arms • sharp, quick nods
Facial Expression	• lifted eyebrows • pleading look • wide-eyed, rapid blinking • nervous or guilty smile • chewing lower lip • shows anger with averted eyes • blushing • guilty look	• relaxed, thoughtful caring or concerned look • few blinks • genuine smile • relaxed mouth • shows anger with flashing eyes, serious look • slight flush or color	• furrowed brow • tight jaw • tense look • patronizing or sarcastic smiles • tight lips
Voice	• quiet, soft, higher pitch • "uh," "ah"s, and hesitations • stopping mid-word • nervous laughter • statements sound like questions with voice tone rising at the end	• resonant, firm, pleasant, smooth even-flowing • comfortable delivery • laughter only with humor • voice tones stay even when making statement	• steely quiet or loud, harsh biting off words • precise measured delivery • sarcastic laughter • statements sound like orders or pronouncements

Assertive Self-Assessment

How assertive are you now? The statements in this pre-assessment represent different assertive characteristics. Check the box that best describes the frequency of your behavior as it relates to each of the statements, using the following scale:

1 – *Never*
2 – *Rarely*
3 – *Sometimes*
4 – *Often*

Behavior	1	2	3	4
1. I use "feeling" talk. I express my personal likes and interests spontaneously. I use the phrases "I feel" or "I think" when it is appropriate.				
2. I make greeting talk. I am outgoing and friendly with people I want to know better. I smile and sound pleased to see them.				
3. I talk about myself. If I do something worthwhile and interesting, I let friends and family know about it. I don't monopolize the conversation, but can mention my accomplishments when it is appropriate.				
4. I accept compliments. I accept compliments graciously. I reward rather than punish the person who complimented me. I give genuine compliments when appropriate.				
5. I use appropriate facial expressions. My facial expressions and voice inflections convey the same feeling my words are conveying. I give direct eye contact when conversing with people.				

Behavior	1	2	3	4
6. I express disagreement. When I disagree with someone, I do not pretend to agree for the sake of keeping peace. I can convey my disagreement without conveying anger.				
7. I continuously improve. I increase my capabilities for tomorrow's challenges. I am a constant learner and develop myself in both informal and formal systems. I do not consider myself above feedback. I ask and thank people for feedback.				
8. I confront reality. I don't avoid the real issues. I take issues head on, even the issues that are not easy to discuss. I address the tough stuff directly. I acknowledge the unsaid and lead out courageously in conversation.				
9. I ask for clarification. If I don't understand directions, instructions, or explanations, I ask for clarification rather than going away confused.				
10. I practice accountability. I hold myself and others accountable. I take responsibility for results. I clearly communicate how I am doing and how others are doing. I don't avoid or shirk responsibility. I don't blame others when things go wrong.				
11. I listen first. I listen before I speak. I listen with my ears, eyes and heart. I find out what the most important behaviors are to the people I am working with. I don't assume I know what matters most to others. I don't presume I have all the answers—or all the questions.				
12. I keep my commitments. I say what I am going to do, then do it. I make commitments carefully and keep them. I don't break confidences and make excuses if I break a commitment.				

Behavior	1	2	3	4
13. I speak up for my rights. I do not let others take advantage of me when I feel put upon. I can say *no* without feeling guilty. I demand my rights and ask to be treated with fairness and justice. I can register my complaints firmly without blowing up.				
14. I am persistent. If I have a legitimate complaint, I continue to restate it despite resistance from the other party until I get satisfaction.				
15. I avoid justifying every opinion. If someone continually argues and asks *why, why, why*, I can stop the questioning by refusing to go along.				
16. I negotiate. I suggest and negotiate mutually satisfying solutions to a variety of interpersonal problems.				

Note. Adapted from Bower & Bower (2004), pp. 4–5.

The key to this assessment is to review the items checked *never* or *rarely*. For self-improvement, set up a work plan moving your *never(s)* to *rarely*, then your *rarely(s)* to *sometimes* and *regularly*.

Submissive (Passive) Behavior

(I lose, you win)

Submissive or passive behavior is described as failing to stand up for one's rights or doing so in an ineffectual way. The submissive goal is to avoid rocking the boat. People who typically behave submissively demonstrate a lack of respect for their own needs and rights. Submissive behavior helps create "lose-win" situations. A person behaving submissively allows others to win. This behavior may lead to being a victim, not a winner.

Submissive Payoffs

- Avoiding conflicts

- Maintaining a familiar pattern of behavior

> *Every relationship involves each person having 50% of the responsibility for the success or failure of the relationship. We cannot be responsible for the thoughts, feelings, opinions, habits, or behaviors of others, but we are responsible for our own.*

- Carrying a smaller load of responsibility

- Gaining the approval of others

- Being looked after and protected by other people

- Controlling others, in a way

Submissive Penalties

- Unfulfilled needs

- Less satisfying relationships

- Affection from others grows old

- Affection toward others tends to wane

- Inability to control one's own emotions

Examples of Submissive Behavior

- Apologizing for things that are not your fault

- Not expressing your needs, opinions, or feelings

- Not respecting your own rights

- Feeling you don't have a right to ask for things you want

- Avoiding conflict, even at your own discomfort

Exercise

Identify a situation in which you exhibited **submissive** behavior. How did you behave? How did you feel?

- Being unable to say *no* to demanding requests without feeling guilty

- Allowing others to control your life, so your life feels out of control

- Taking responsibility for the actions of others—convincing yourself that you were probably at fault to begin with.

Passive-Aggressive Behavior

(I lose, you win)

This behavior is another "I lose, you win" style—a passive expression of negative sentiments, feelings of anger, and resentfulness. So instead of verbally or physically expressing frustration or anger or even saying *no* when asked to complete a task, you may simply act agreeable, expressing your negative feelings in a covert style with passive resistance. You choose not to ask for or act on what you want. You may often use procrastination, inefficiency, and forgetfulness to avoid doing what you need to do or have been told by others to do.

Examples of Passive-Aggressive Behavior

- Performing a requested action too late to be helpful

- Performing it in a way that is useless

- Sabotaging the action to show anger that you cannot express in words

- Avoiding responsibility by claiming forgetfulness

- Blaming others

- Sulking

- Dealing with needs, opinions, and feelings by NOT dealing with them

- Apologizing but secretly resenting it, perhaps using sarcasm

- Respecting the rights of others but resenting it, secretly sabotaging progress

- Often functioning as a victim in learned helplessness

- Avoiding conflict in an indirect way (muttering under your breath, dirty looks, slamming doors, etc.)

Exercise

Identify a situation in which you exhibited **passive-aggressive** behavior. How did you behave? How did you feel?

Aggressive Behavior

(I win, you lose)

Aggressive behavior is more complex. Aggressive behavior is standing up for oneself by putting other people down. It can be active or passive, direct or indirect, honest or dishonest—but the goal is always to win by communicating an impression of superiority and disrespectfulness. By being aggressive you put your wants, needs, and rights above those of others. You attempt to get your way by not allowing others a choice. Aggressive behavior is usually effective by making sure others "lose"—but in doing so, aggressive people set themselves up for retaliation. No one likes a bully!

Aggressive Behavior Payoffs

- Likely to secure the materials needed and objects desired
- Protects self and personal space
- Helps to retain control over one's own life and the lives of others

Aggressive Penalties

- Increased fear of retaliation
- Creates its own opposition and fosters destruction
- Results in loss of control
- Dehumanizes the aggressor
- Creates pangs of guilt

Examples of Aggressive Behavior

- Not respecting needs, opinions, or feelings of others

- Not apologizing for things, even when at fault

- Feeling as though others do not have a right to ask for things they want

- Avoiding one's own discomfort, even at the risk of conflict

- Having an inflated sense of entitlement, as though the world owes them

- Controlling of others in order to feel in control of their own life

- Not taking responsibility for one's own actions

> ### *Exercise*
> Identify a situation in which you exhibited **aggressive** behavior. How did you behave? How did you feel?

Assertive Behavior

(I win, you win)

Assertive behavior is described as standing up for one's rights without violating the rights of others. The goal of assertion is to find a mutual solution and give straight communication. Behaving with appropriate assertion increases the likelihood of success in human interaction.

Assertive behavior is active, direct, and honest. It communicates an impression of self-respect and respect for others. By being assertive we view our wants, needs, and rights as equal with those of others. An assertive person works toward "win-win" outcomes by influencing, listening, and negotiating so that others willingly choose to cooperate. This behavior leads to success without retaliation and encourages honest, open relationships.

Assertive Behavior Payoffs

- Helps build positive self-esteem
- Fosters fulfilling relationships

- Reduces fear and anxiety
- Improves chances of getting desired results
- Satisfies needs

Assertive Penalties

- Negative results may occur
- May get hurt
- Difficult to alter ingrained habits

> ## Exercise
>
> Identify a situation in which you exhibited **assertive** behavior. How did you behave? How did you feel?

Examples of Assertive Behavior

- Respecting needs, opinions, and feelings, both their own and others'
- Apologizing when at fault, but allowing others to take responsibility for their own actions as well
- Respecting one's own rights and the rights of others
- Asking for things one needs or wants
- Dealing with conflict in healthy ways
- Being mature enough to take responsibility for oneself
- Approaching conflict from a position of respect and trying to seek out a win/win situation for all involved
- Establishing a solid set of boundaries for oneself and communicating them clearly
- Respecting the boundaries of others
- Being aware of one's strengths and weaknesses, and accepting both
- Not being manipulative
- Feeling in control of one's life

Assertion is a choice. A major goal of assertion is to enable people to take charge of their own lives. It helps them break out of ruts and away from stereotyped or compulsive behaviors. At its best, assertion helps people develop the power of choice over their actions. Sometimes it is wise to give in to others, and sometimes it may be necessary to aggressively defend one's rights. Therefore, the ultimate goal of assertion is to help people choose their behaviors effectively, not have them behave assertively in every situation.

Basic Assertive Guidelines

- Actively listen.
- Use "I" statements rather than "you" statements.
- Attack the problem, not the person.
- Use factual descriptions instead of judgments or exaggerations.
- Express thoughts, feelings and opinions reflecting ownership.
- Use clear, direct requests or directives when you want others to do something rather than hinting, being indirect, or presuming.
- Stay focused.
- Practice, practice, practice.

All of us use the following four delivery styles, depending on the situation and personal factors.

Four Assertive Delivery Styles

1. **Supportive/Caring**: Using warm, mellow tone of voice. Communicating personal interest, appreciation, concern, gratitude, or empathy by making good eye contact and using comforting facial expressions (e.g., smiles) and vocabulary.

"If you can spare the time, will you please give me some help on this project? Thank you so much."

2. **Directive/Guiding**: Being firm and authoritative but not harsh or dictatorial. The delivery should be matter-of-fact, direct, and serious. The facial expression is one of concentration or purpose.

"You did a good job on the meeting arrangements."

3. **Analytical**: Using an even, no-nonsense, pragmatic delivery. The facial expression looks alert and thoughtful. It means being polite but not showing a lot of emotion.

"Your arrangements for the conference were very thorough. The sessions were on time and the handouts and speakers were informative."

4. **Expressive**: Being enthusiastic in voice and gestures. The voice range and facial expressions are limitless. Being animated and showing emotion with the face, the hands, and body movements.

"Super job! Great presentation!"

Which Is Which?

Identify the behavior style (submissive, aggressive, passive-aggressive, or assertive) that each of following statements represents. See page 243 for the answers.

1. "Only an idiot would think of a solution like that! Don't you ever think before you talk?"

2. "This is probably a dumb idea, but . . ."

3. "Well, okay, if that's what you want to do. I don't care."

4. "This probably isn't what you wanted, but I guess I wasn't too sure about what you said and, anyway, I am not good at this kind of thing."

5. "When you don't take accurate telephone messages, I feel frustrated because . . ."

6. "Just shut up! You talk too much."

7. "I get upset when you call me that."

8. "Thanks for inviting me, but I'm really not into Thai food."

9. "You really upset me when you say that!"

The skill of listening becomes very important in assertive communication.

We Listen Through Filters

Listening is a very important skill. In a typical day, we spend about 40% listening. It is important to remember that everything we hear and say is filtered in our minds through our life experiences. While we are listening through our filters, the other person is also listening through theirs.

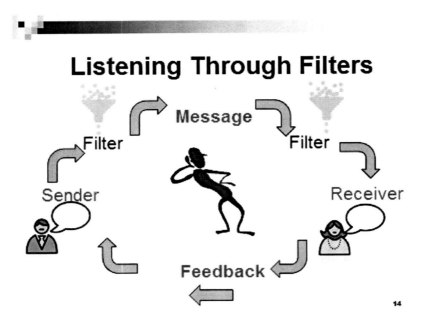

Our experiences in life influence our behavior. Your behaviors have shaped your beliefs, and your beliefs impact the way you filter information. You may not always hear information in the same way as others. Your filters are affected by:

past experiences	beliefs
attitudes	values
prejudices	expectations
assumptions	strong feelings
interests	memories

Your Listening Habits

Put a check (✓) by each item on this list that *annoys you the most*. Add your own items to the list if you think of others.

Put an asterisk (*) after each behavior on this list that *is most important to you* when someone is listening to you.

☐ Daydreaming
☐ Discounting information
☐ Jumping to conclusions
☐ Interrupting
☐ Ignoring
☐ Losing eye contact
☐ Finishing speaker's thoughts
☐ Changing the subject
☐ Excessive physical activity
☐ Habitually challenging/defying the speaker

Based on the above checkmarks and asterisks, list the areas that you want to improve and how you will do it.

1. Area:

   I will _____.

2. Area:

   I will _____.

3. Area:

   I will _____.

4. Area:

   I will _____.

Assertive Listening Skills to Develop

Using minimum encouragements: Simple verbal and nonverbal responses encourage the speaker to talk in his or her own way and also keep the listener active. Minimum encouragements are brief indicators to the speaker that you are still with him or her.

- *Use verbal prompts*:

  "Uh huh, tell me more."

  "What else has happened?"

  "Mm-hmm. I see."

  "Please continue."

  "Really?"

  "Go on."

- *Repeat key words*: Repeating the last few words of the person's last sentence.

- *Give nonverbal cues*: Using signals that encourage the other person to continue talking, e.g., good eye contact, supportive and increased facial expressions, nods, leaning forward.

- *Use silence*: Waiting for the other person to respond and talk. Pauses need not be embarrassing. By not filling the void, you let the person know that you are listening and are interested in what he or she is saying and that you expect a response.

Paraphrasing or restating: Carefully listen, and then rephrase in your own words the essence of what the speaker has said. This concise response is most effective (1) when there are arguments, (2) at the onset of a conversation, and (3) when you've just received complicated information or instructions.

Questioning: A question can be a response that indicates that your intent is to gather further information, providing further discussion along a certain line. It implies that the other person needs to discuss or develop a point further. Questions can be used to surface both positive and negative information. Questioning for more negative information is appropriate when the other person feels comfortable and not threatened.

- *Open-ended questions* cannot be answered with a simple "yes" or "no" response. These usually begin with words like *who, what, where, how*, and sometimes *why*. Think of open-ended questions as essay questions.
- *Closed-ended questions* tend to be answered briefly by a single word such as *yes* or *no*. Think of closed-ended questions as true-or-false or multiple-choice questions.
- *Follow-on* or *leading-into* questions build upon and respond to answers. For instance, "Tell me more about that," and "Based upon that, what do you feel about . . . ?"

The mirror technique: Restate what the other person said in your own words, with an implied question at the end.

Speaker: "You never told me it was due today!"

You, *mirroring*: "I never told you it was due today . . . ?"

Mirroring is most effective when the other person has become angry or defensive or when one wants to generate more dialogue.

Reflecting: Identify the speaker's feelings and verbalize them succinctly. This allows you to check for the accuracy of your own perceptions and lets the speaker know that he or she is being understood. It affirms the speaker's feelings and encourages him or her to continue or elaborate. When feelings and facts are joined in one succinct response, we have a reflection of meaning. Your reflection of the other person's feelings involves mirroring back to the speaker, in concise statements, the emotions you think he or she is communicating.

Speaker: "My supervisor keeps asking questions about my personal life. I wish she would mind her business."

You, *reflecting*: "You feel annoyed that she won't respect your privacy."

Assertive Word Choice

Many people have been taught to think it is impolite, inappropriate, or pushy to be direct and honest about their feelings. However, sometimes we are so careful we really don't communicate the real message we want to convey. To communicate thoughts, feelings, and opinions assertively, you need to choose words that are direct, honest, appropriate, and respectful. Some words simply do not fit these criteria and cannot be delivered assertively. While words are only one aspect of being assertive, your vocabulary is important in conveying your message. This may seem "picky," but consider the following:

> ## Tips for Active Listening
>
> - Don't interrupt
> - Don't just listen for the words; listen for feeling and meaning
> - Test for understanding by paraphasing or summarizing before responding
> - Ask questions
> - Acknowledge feelings
> - Use silence—sometimes it is best to just keep your mouth shut!

Which sounds more assertive? "Don't you think . . . ?" or "I think that . . ."

Which sounds more assertive? "Why don't you . . . ?" Or "Will you . . . ?"

1.   Use "I" statements to transform aggression to assertion:

"You embarrassed me in front of all those people." (Aggressive)

"<u>I felt embarrassed</u> when you said that in front of all those people." (Assertive)

"You always interrupt me when I am giving my presentations at the meetings!" (Aggressive)

"<u>I would like</u> to give my presentations without interruption." (Assertive)

Instead of . . .	*You could say:*
1. You make me sick.	_____
2. You sure are bossy.	_____
3. You always embarrass me.	_____
4. You make me mad.	_____
5. You are never on time.	_____

2. Use factual descriptions.

"This is sloppy work." (Aggressive)

"The punctuation in your report needs work. Also, the headings are spaced inconsistently." (Aggressive)

"If you don't change your attitude, you're going to be in big trouble." (Aggressive)

"If you continue to arrive after 8:00 a.m., I will be required to ask you to submit a leave slip for the time." (Assertive)

3. Express thoughts, feelings, and opinions reflecting ownership.

"Don't you think we should table this action for now?" (Submissive, indirect, no ownership)

"I think tabling this action would allow us more time to gather data." (Assertive, shows ownership of thought)

"She makes me mad!" (Submissive, denies ownership of feelings)

"I get angry when she breaks her promises." (Assertive, owns feelings)

4. Use clear, direct requests (commands) when you want others to do something rather than hinting, being indirect, or presuming.

"Would you mind taking this to Dianne?" (Indirect, inquires only about willingness)

"Will you please pick up a copy of the report when you go?" (Assertive request)

"I need five copies of this for my meeting." (Presumes the other will make copies when need is verbalized, does not direct or ask for help)

"Please make five copies of this for my meeting." (Assertive directive)

Expressing your honest emotions is not always easy. First you must identify the feeling. Based on the four basic human emotions, are you mad, sad, glad, or scared? Some feelings are a combination of two or more of the four categories. This is just a small sampling of emotions that are used in assertive messages.

Mad	*Glad*	*Sad*	*Scared*	*Combination*
upset	pleased	unhappy	anxious	guilty
irritated	happy	disappointed	worried	frustrated
annoyed	delighted	hurt	fearful	embarrassed
angry	comfortable	down	concerned	uncomfortable
furious	excited	despondent	afraid	confused
miffed	grateful	depressed	nervous	torn
ticked off	appreciative	diminished	alarmed	self-conscious
irate				humiliated
stifled				insignificant

Manipulative Barriers to Assertive Behavior

Don't think that because you are practicing your assertiveness skills that people will not try to manipulate you. Listed below are a few ways people may try to counteract your assertive message and behavior. Remember to stand your ground. Focus on your message and goal.

Rapid Take-Over: The person tries to or takes over the conversation to divert your attention from the real issue.

Flattery: The person uses complimentary remarks or attention to get his or her way.

Over-the-Barrel: The person closes the whole range of options with "take it or leave it."

Labeling: The person inaccurately describes, classifies, or stereotypes you.

Guilt Induction: The person attempts to have you do something by making you feel guilty.

Helplessness: The person appeals to your strengths and focuses on your weaknesses to get something done.

Apologizing Blamelessly

Most people, when angry, are sensitive and their feelings are easily hurt. An apology should be blameless in order to prevent a new focus for the negativity or the anger. For example: Don't say "I'm sorry the supervisor has ignored your request." Instead, say "I'm sorry. I know how frustrating it is when things like this happen."

Some Tips for Handling Critical Feedback

Remember: You can't do better until you know better!

Seek feedback on projects or assignments before miscommunication occurs and mistakes become a crisis for the supervisor or project leader.

1. Ask trusted coworkers and colleagues for positive feedback if none is ever offered. An example might be, "What do you especially like about how I handled the project?"

2. Listen carefully to your critic to make sure you understand the critical feedback. Repeat back. Request that the critic be specific.

3. Don't automatically assume your critic is right or wrong. Take the time to assess whether or not the feedback is valid before taking any action. Ask questions to clarify the feedback or get specific examples of where you were wrong.

4. Evaluate the source of the feedback and whether it was offered constructively. Does the feedback give action to consider? Is it future-oriented? Or is it offered destructively, with words such as *always, never,* and *should*? Is it focused on the past?

5. Do not become a silent victim or passively accept critical feedback. Show self-confidence.

6. When you have made a mistake, avoid being too apologetic or overcompensating. Admit your errors rather than trying to cover them up.

7. Don't make exaggerated negative assessments about your own character or ability based on one mistake, such as "I'm so stupid" or "I'll never be any good at this." Give yourself credit for past victories and accomplishments.

8. Lower your emotional temperature when dealing with critical feedback by use of positive self-talk such as "I'm okay; I may have made a mistake, but learning from this will increase my skills."

9. Ask for or offer a solution to the issue or problem.

Giving Constructive Feedback

When to give constructive feedback?

- A coworker is not functioning well
- A situation is threatening the working relationship with a coworker

- There is a sincere desire to improve a coworker's performance for the good of the organization
- A project or idea requires improvement or modification

The objectives of constructive feedback are

- To correct or improve a problematic situation, coworker's performance, or problems with ideas or projects
- To secure a positive response from the receiving the feedback

> ### Keep a "Me" File
>
> Keep a file with examples of your work that you are especially proud of, such as letters of appreciation, awards, newspaper clippings, and notes and e-mails of congratulations you have received. Review your "me" file when you are feeling down and need an encouraging boost because of others' critical feedback.

Before you give feedback, make certain the situation really calls for it. Make sure your feedback is motivated by a genuine problem or issue, not by your personal dislikes or frustrations. Most of all, make certain that the problem or issue is serious enough to warrant feedback.

Feedback Criteria

- Describe, in a nonjudgmental way, specific behavior and observable actions, not general or subjective behavior.
- Address only one issue at a time.
- Consider the receiver's feelings—focus on the value and usefulness the feedback may provide the receiver, not on the release it provides you.
- Express feelings, so long as you direct them toward the behavior and not the person.
- Request alternatives—be proactive. State what you would like the person to do instead.
- Choose the time and situation for the feedback strategically. Try to do it as soon as possible, but not in the heat of the moment unless you can maintain your composure. Avoid public discussion unless it is an issue for the entire team.
- Follow up with positive feedback if the situation improves or the issue is corrected.

Writing Assertive Scripts for Constructive Feedback

Planning is a key step. Writing out your script

- gives you a concrete task as a starting point toward assertion;
- forces you to clarify the situation and define your needs, so you stop and think objectively about your actions;
- gives you confidence in handling the next confrontation assertively because you know what you want, avoiding stupid, thoughtless outbursts you will later regret; and
- helps you find the exact words to express what you want, so you have a written record of your planned message that you can review for effectiveness instead of relying on your memory.

Use the following methodology as a guide to giving constructive feedback.

The Awareness Wheel

The Awareness Wheel illustrates a six-step method to address inappropriate behavior in an assertive way. You begin the script by objectively describing the specific behavior you find bothersome or do not want. The second step is to be empathetic if possible; try to see the situation from the other person's perspective. The third step is to express what you feel and think when the behavior or situation occurs. The fourth step is describing the behavior you want; you ask explicitly for a different, specific behavior. In the fifth step, you spell out the consequences (payoffs and penalties) to the individual, emphasizing the positive consequences first. The final step is coming to closure through discussion and an agreement.

1. **Observation/Description**—Describe the behavior you do not want: "I would like to discuss," "I see," "I have observed," "I have noticed"

Describe exactly what and how you see the other person's present behavior as objectively as possible. Use concrete terms and examples; specify the time, place, and frequency of the behaviors and actions. Describe the action, not the motive.

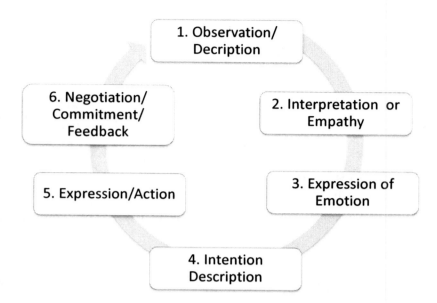

"The punctuation in this report needs work: commas are not placed properly and there are numerous run-on sentences. For example, look at . . ."

"I have noticed that for the last two days you have used the speakerphone in your cubicle for your personal calls."

2. **Interpretation or Empathy**—Show understanding: "I think," "I can imagine"

Show some understanding of the other's position; be honest, not sarcastic.

"I can imagine that you were busy and you did not catch it."

"I can see how you didn't think it was a big deal or that it wouldn't bother me."

3. **Expression of Emotion**—Express feelings: "I feel," "I get"

Calmly express how the behavior or actions make you think and feel. Express your thoughts in a positive manner related to the goal. Direct your comments to the specific offending behavior or action, not the whole person

"I get frustrated when it happens."

"I feel embarrassed when I hear your personal information."

4.   Intention—Request alternative behavior: "I want," "I do not want"

State explicitly the desired changes in behavior you want or would like to see. Specify the concrete action you want to see stopped and those you want to see started. Request only one or two small changes at a time. Specify (only if appropriate) what behavior you are willing to change to make the agreement.

"I want you to review your report before you turn it over to me."

"I want you find a more private place for your personal conversations."

5.   Expression/Action—Identify consequences, results: "I will"

Explain what you will do if there is change in behavior. Positive consequences are desirable; however, if there are none, explain the negative consequences or punishment if the behavior continues. You are more likely to succeed by emphasizing the positive, rewarding consequences for the desired behavior, than by dwelling on the negative consequences for undesirable behavior. Always select a consequence that you are willing to carry out.

"If you can do this I will have no problems working with you on this project."

"If you do this I know we can work better together."

6.   Negotiation/Commitment/Feedback—Request feedback: "Let's talk about this," "I would like your feedback"

Ask if you can talk about how you can get the behavior you want.

"I would like to hear from you on how I can get you to do this."

"I would like to talk about how I can get you to . . ."

Assertive Statement Scripts

Practice asserting yourself by creating a statement for the following situations, using the guiding phrases "I see," "I feel," "I want," "I will," and "Let's talk about" to construct your script. Suggested responses are on page 243.

1. Your coworker has a habit of coming behind you in your cubicle and rubbing your shoulders and back. You are very uncomfortable when they do it, but have not said anything so far.

I see . . .

I think . . .

I feel . . .

I want . . .

I will . . .

I want your feedback on . . . (or) Let's talk about . . .

2. At the organization where you work, you are irritated with your supervisor because she has not explained all your duties. What's your script for approaching her?

I see . . .

I think . . .

I feel . . .

I want . . .

I will . . .

I want your feedback on . . . (or) Let's talk about . . .

3. You have been quiet about your coworker's habit of interrupting your speaking because you carpool together and you want to keep the peace. What's your script for approaching him?

I see . . .

I think . . .

I feel . . .

I want . . .

I will . . .

I want your feedback on . . . (or) Let's talk about . . .

Applying the Awareness Wheel

Identify a work-related situation that you would like to use with the Awareness Wheel method. Write out the situation and describe the behaviors or practices that the person engages in that really upset or bug you. Describe how these behaviors impact your ability to perform at your best. Write out your script in the space below.

Four Basic Skills of Assertive Behavior

The Broken Record

- The calm repetition of your position, desire, or intention, given in a low-level, relaxed voice

- It allows you to stick to the point by ignoring manipulative verbal side traps, argument baiting, and irrelevant logic. You remain focused on your goal without giving up or losing your temper.

- Select a concise one-sentence refusal statement and only use that statement, no matter what the other person says.

- After each statement by the other person, say your broken-record sentence. Do not allow yourself to get sidetracked by responding to any other raised issues.

- Say it in a soft, calm, unemotional voice.

- Allow plenty of silence. Silence will help the other person realize that all the statements and manipulations will be futile.

- Persist. Simply state your broken-record refusal one more time than the other person's request, questions, or statements. If they have five interactions, you need to give six broken-record statements.

Responses: *"No, I do not want to go." "No, I do not want to buy . . ."*

Fogging

- Admitting you might be wrong
- The calm acknowledgment of the possibility that there may be some truth in the critical feedback given; like a fog bank, you are unaffected by manipulative criticism.
- It allows you to receive criticism without becoming anxious or defensive.
- Just listen to the statement and agree with any truth or any possible logic—don't be defensive.

> Responses: *"You could be right about that." "What you said makes sense." "You might be right about my defensiveness."*

Practice Fogging

Write a response to each scenario below, using the fogging technique.

1. A coworker tells you "You talk too much!"

2. A coworker complains to you that you always seem to get what you want from the supervisor. "What's the deal?"

3. A female colleague says to you, "Just like a man—so unemotional."

4. A male colleague says to you, "Just like a woman—so emotional."

Negative Assertion

- Admitting errors or mistakes
- Desensitizes the criticism
- Once you accept the mistake, you can move forward.

Responses: *"You're right. I didn't complete the report on time and this is what I am planning to do next month to ensure the report is timely." "You're right. I probably didn't think it through carefully. Do you have any suggestions as to how I can improve?"*

Think of a situation at work where you know you were wrong. Could you have handled it better? Write out a negative assertive statement that you could have used in the situation.

Negative Inquiry

- The active prompting of criticism by listening to your critic and asking questions to elicit his or her feelings and thoughts.
- You gain information that you can use, and you exhaust your critic's complaint.

Responses: *"How could I have contributed more?" "Could you please give me some examples?" "What specifically did I do?"*

Think of a situation at work in which you knew you were being criticized. Could you have handled it better? In the space below, write out a negative inquiry statement that you could have used in the situation.

> ### Handling a Put-Down
>
> - Ignore it
> - Respond with a direct, assertive statement: "Please don't call me a 'good girl.' I am offended by that remark."
> - Respond in kind with a witty reply. Remark: "You did a great job, considering you're a woman." Reply: "For a man, you didn't do too bad, either."

Tips for Handling Difficult Behaviors

1. Try to stay calm and matter-of-fact in your tone, facial expressions, body stance, and word choices.

2. Use "double think." Continually try to look at the situation from both your point of view and the other person's point of view. Hang on to your determination, but add an understanding of the other side's needs and feelings.

3. Spend as much time as you can on preparation. Do your homework on both your side and their side. Write out an assertive script.

4. Spend time asking questions and gathering information.

5. Be honest. Point out the difficult behavior or tactic that is being used.

6. Avoid putting yourself or others in corners with public statements with no escape clauses, threats, ultimatums, humiliation, or loss-of-face attacks.

When you back people into corners, they will believe that they have only two choices, flight or fight. Most people fight.

When You Don't Know What To Say . . .

When you can't remember a technique or you can't think of anything clearly appropriate to say, you can:

Be frank. You don't always need quick remarks to make people aware of how much they have hurt you: "Ouch, that really hurt."

Say nothing. Saying nothing and walking away is an honorable response to an insulting question or statement.

Repeat the offending question or statement. Repetition forces the person to hear how ridiculous or out-of-line the statement was, and can sometimes force the person to apologize.

Use kindness or humor. If the question or statement isn't too insensitive or upsetting and the relationship is worth preserving, kindness and humor may serve you best.

Self-Fulfilling Prophecy and Assertiveness

As discussed in Chapter 8, the *self-fulfilling prophecy* is a well-documented phenomenon. Many people would agree that the common use of the term translates to attitude about events to come. The self-fulfilling prophecy is any positive or negative expectation about circumstances, events, or people that may affect a person's behavior in a manner that causes the expectation to be fulfilled. For example, a person stating "I'm probably going to have a lousy day" might unwittingly approach every situation that day with a negative attitude and see only problems, thus fulfilling the prediction of a lousy day. Or, vice-versa, a person who espouses a self-fulfilling prophecy in a positive way, believing "I'm going to have a great day," might act in ways that will actually make this prediction true. In most cases, this is a subconscious gesture.

How does this relate to being assertive? Assertive behavior comes more naturally when you believe you can be more assertive. Analyze the messages you are giving yourself. If they are continuously negative, based on "I can't" statements, you need to reprogram your thinking. It is important that you believe you can and will get the results you want. So practice, practice, practice.

Chapter 10
Now You're the Boss!

"Just remember: People tend to resist that which is forced upon them. People tend to support that which they help to create." —Vince Pfaff

Now you are the boss. You said you would do it differently from your boss—but how? What is your new game plan? How do you make the transition from the employee to the supervisor? This chapter cannot take the place of formal supervisory training, but it can give you insights into successfully making the transition to supervision. It identifies many of the roles, responsibilities, personal traits, and interpersonal skills that lead to successful leadership as a supervisor.

Successful supervisors have certain personal skills that make them stand out from the crowd of employees. Those skills, often referred to as "style," lead to self-confidence, which in turn causes others to have confidence in you. This phenomenon is fairly universal. You must handle yourself and your job in a way that makes others want to be a part of your team.

From Technical Expert to Supervisor

Technical Expert	Supervisor
• Focuses on single issues with clearly defined parameters	• Focuses on multiple issues, some of which are ill-defined
• Works in knowledge areas where he or she has great education and experience	• Works in many areas, often with little training and varying degrees of experience
• Can analyze details and consider a range of connections and implications	• Must look at broad perspectives and identify high-impact issues quickly
• Is recognized as an expert who provides technical answers and suggests actions	• Is seen as a generalist who must make decisions effectively and get good results

The Basic Work of Supervision

- Assign and distribute work
- Monitor and control performance
- Review and evaluate performance
- Train and develop employees
- Lead the group
- Communicate to group and management
- Handle administrative duties
- Provide leadership

Responsibilities of Supervision

- Responsibility to management
- Responsibility to your work group
- Responsibility to yourself

Attitude Is Your Key to Success!

No matter what you may do to hide it, your attitude will be showing. Nothing will improve relationships with those you supervise more than a consistently positive attitude on your part. Your attitude sets the tone and pace in your workplace. There is a direct relationship between your attitude and the productivity of those you supervise. When you are upbeat, your employees will respond in positive ways that will enhance productivity. **When you are negative, expect a drop in productivity.**

"Find ways to convince your people that you see them all as either winners or potential winners and you mean them no harm. When you do, you will find that communication within your organization is greatly enhanced."

—Ken Blanchard, *Leadership Smarts*

Self-Assessment of Supervisory Competencies

Put a check (✓) next to the competencies you think you possess, then answer the questions that follow.

- ☐ **Self-awareness:** Awareness of personal core values, life and professional goals, and strengths and weaknesses

- ☐ **Decisiveness/courage**: Ability to take a stand and withstand opposition, pressure, and difficulties when necessary

- ☐ **Political savvy**: Understanding of the factors that affect decision making and ability to use formal and informal processes and networking positively to influence decisions and achieve worthy goals

- ☐ **Developing others**: Interest and ability to help others develop greater knowledge and skills

- ☐ **Stress management**: Ability to handle pressure effectively and act professionally at all times

- ☐ **Technical knowledge:** Effectiveness in carrying out all technical aspects of the job

- ☐ **Tolerance:** Ability to work with divergent views, personalities, and cultures

- ☐ **People skills:** Effectiveness in relating to others positively in all situations

- ☐ **Communication skills**: Ability to convey information effectively orally and in writing

- ☐ **Resilience:** Ability to handle difficulties and setbacks and remain positive and fully engaged

- ☐ **Creativity:** Ability to develop new approaches to solve problems or take initiative

- ☐ **Planning and managing projects and finances:** Ability to apply proven principles of project management, cost control, and staying within a budget

Which competencies do you think are your strongest?

Which competencies do you think you need to develop more?

How will you plan for your development in these competencies?

Making the Transition From Employee to Supervisor

Establishing Your Authority

- Get acquainted—meet with everyone in the group (first week), identify informal leaders.

- Set a positive tone.

- Stay warm and friendly with former coworkers but slowly back away. You cannot be a supervisor and a buddy at the same time.

- Do not permit those who were coworkers yesterday to intimidate you today. If you play favorites, you are in trouble.

- Do what you can to make everyone's job better than it was before you became supervisor. Do not make the same mistakes your boss made when you were an employee.

- Demonstrate to your previous coworkers that you are knowledgeable by teaching them, in a sensitive manner, new skills that will make their jobs easier.

- Seek more assistance from your supervisor in making your transition. Ask for suggestions. Be a good listener.

- Give previous coworkers credit when credit is due.

- Don't assume anything.

Ways to Establish Credibility

- Be yourself

- Be decisive

- Keep your cool

- Be fair

- Be firm when necessary

Ways of Working Through Others

- Clarify expectations

- Provide feedback

- Provide opportunity

- Threaten punishment

- Offer reward

- Appeal to values

Stages in Team Development

Chapter 7, "Working in Groups," discussed the stages of group development as they relate to individual group members. In this section, the fives stages are further expanded to help new supervisors ease into their role as group leaders.

To recap, the five stages of development that have been identified are: **(1) forming, (2) storming, (3) norming, (4) performing,** and **(5) adjourning.**

Stage 1: Forming

1. **Ensure team members really get to know one another.** Provide a process for in-depth introductions if team members don t know one another. If they do

know each other, but have not worked in this team before, offer a process by which they can begin sharing their values about the work at hand, for example:

- "As we introduce ourselves, please describe what you would like to see come out of this team experience."

- "After we have introduced ourselves, let's develop a joint statement—a few sentences—about what we will be able to accomplish as a team that might not have been accomplished, or not accomplished as well, if we were doing this work as individuals."

2. **Establish ground rules**—operational, process, and behavioral.

   Examples of **Operational** ground rules:

   - Meet once a week on Thursdays at 10:00 in the second-floor conference room.

   - Hold meetings to one hour unless all participants agree to extend the time and can stay.

   - Rotate recorder and timekeeper roles among members.

   - Circulate a record of decisions made within one week of the meeting.

   Examples of **Process** ground rules:

   - Make decisions by consensus (everyone agrees to follow the plan, etc.).

   - Take a consensus poll by a showing of thumbs: thumbs up for "agree with," thumbs to the side for "can live with," and thumbs down for "cannot live with."

   Examples of **Behavioral** ground rules:

   - Listen to and respect others' experiences, ideas, concerns, and insights.

- Be candid—put real issues on the table, including areas of disagreement.

- Actively seek consensus—look for common ground, be open to compromise, offer consensus proposals.

- Deal with issues affecting the team—don't complain outside of the team.

- Speak one at a time; raise your hand to be called on if discussion gets heated.

3. **Create feelings of inclusion**—use nonjudgmental, supportive language and behavior. For example:

- Acknowledge and reinforce different thinking and working styles in a positive way vs. expecting all team members to adopt a particular narrow set of beliefs or practices.

- Respond to challenges in a receptive, nondefensive manner, establishing an open dialogue for all members of the team vs. closing off discussion of concerns expressed by some members.

- Support each person on the team, especially when outlying views are expressed or special needs or problems emerge vs. allowing any individuals to become isolated on the team.

Stage 2: Storming

1. **Deal with differences openly.** Bring differences out into the open; use the ground rules to encourage different points of view to be expressed, listened to, and respected.

2. **Handling issues affecting the team, in the team.** Help the team explore differences in their individual backgrounds so differences in point of view can be understood in context.

3. **Involve all team members in resolving issues.** For example, when issues about the team's work are raised by one or a few people, encourage the whole team to help define, analyze, and resolve the issues. Encourage the team work out its issues together, and not to bring up complaints or disagreements outside of the team.

4. **Have team members work together in mixed and changing subgroups.** Propose opportunities for team members to work with each other in various combinations; for example, create subgroups for different activities or tasks. This will give everyone a chance to get to know and trust all other members of the team.

Stage 3: Norming

1. **Get the team to agree explicitly on what it is trying to achieve.** Have team members develop a consensus statement of the team's vision, mission, or common purpose early on. At the start of each meeting or each new task, have team members discuss what the objectives are for that specific situation.

2. **Help the team develop common values.** For example, lead a discussion on the importance of the project at hand, possible positive outgrowths of their efforts, or what would make this project or effort the biggest possible success. The team may also benefit from a discussion of what a team is, so that they can establish common values about themselves as a team.

3. **Create opportunities for shared experiences.** Provide chances for team members to (a) develop their understanding of issues together, for example, making site visits or attending expert presentations; (b) perform tasks together, for example, making assignments to subgroups rather than individuals; or (c) evaluate team progress together.

4. **Offer opportunities to take risks together.** For example, if the team is to make a presentation to higher management about the team's work, encourage them to do it together. Or if a particularly difficult project has to be undertaken, have them do it, or at least plan it, together.

Stage 4: Performing

1. **Acknowledge skills.** Continue to express confidence and trust in each members competence and motivation regarding task and relationship accomplishments.

2. **Set challenging but realistic goals.** Increase levels of the team's expectations for its performance; for example, higher quality, timeliness, or quantity (if measurable) of work.

3. **Be vigilant about keeping channels of communication open.** Allow for pertinent interchanges of relevant information.

4. **Celebrate as a team.** Provide opportunities for recognition of outstanding team achievements.

Stage 5: Adjourning

Teams deal best with this stage if members know when their work together will conclude. However, this is not always possible. Some approaches that help bring effective closure:

1. **Recognize participation and achievement** provided by the team itself or by the sponsoring organization.

2. **Create opportunities for members to say personal good-byes**, particularly if members are unlikely to work closely together again after the team disbands.

The basis for healthy group development is trust. Without trust, a group will never reach the fourth stage, at least at the optimal level. A developed group may need to begin the entire process over again when trust is broken, or as the group members, work, and organizational policies change.

Management Style

(How do you operate in managing your responsibilities?)

"Trust is established through action."
—Hank Paulson, Chairman and CEO, Goldman Sachs

There is no best way to supervise your group in terms of a hard set of rules that can be religiously followed to yield predictable results. There will be a wide variance in the amount of supervision required for all the personality and ability factors in your group.

In addition, your own personality plays a significant role in how you manage the people you supervise. From a practical standpoint, the best management style is a combination of "hands-on" and "hands-off" management. Some employees may be quite capable of getting their jobs done with minimum supervision. Others may require regular monitoring and guidance. Recognizing these differences and managing to the capabilities of these individual traits is one of the keys to successful supervision.

Relationship Trust Behaviors: A Checklist

Review the definitions from Steven M. R. Covey's book *The Speed of Trust* (pp. 125–232), or go to www.speedoftrust.com, before you begin this exercise. Read each behavior. You may be surprised by each definintion's pros and cons. Check the box that best describes your behavior as it relates to each of the statements. What are the implications for you? If you would like to create a plan of action, use the chart on pages 231–232 in *The Speed of Trust*.

Behavior	*Never*	*Rarely*	*Sometimes*	*Regularly*
I talk straight.				
I demonstrate respect.				

Behavior	Never	Rarely	Sometimes	Regularly
I have no hidden agendas.				
I right my wrongs.				
I show loyalty.				
I deliver results.				
I continuously improve.				
I confront reality.				
I clarify my expectations.				
I practice accountability.				
I listen first.				
I keep my commitments.				
I extend trust.				

Note. Adapted from Stephen M. R. Covey (2006), *The Speed of Trust: The One Thing That Changes Everything.* New York, NY: Free Press.

Are there any insights? What behaviors might you need to move to the "regularly" column? What steps might you take? Action plan?

Holding Others Accountable

- Encourage as much employee involvement as possible

- Ensure that there is clear understanding between you and the employee

- Deliver feedback constructively, objectively and unemotionally, avoiding emotionally charged statements

- Describe the behavior you want changed and offer examples

- Use "I messages" when delivering feedback

- Applaud the employee when giving positive feedback

- Be direct and tactful, and focus on facts

- Make sure the feedback is given in a timely manner

- Balance the negative

- Communicate the impact of the employee's behavior on the employee, you, the rest of the team and the organization

Types of Feedback to Employees

Informative feedback is straightforward information. It does not include any judgment of *good* or *bad*. Common examples include total production figures, suggestions from customers for improvement, number and types of complaints, and number and types of on-the-job injuries.

Reinforcing feedback has a positive quality factor built in. It is an excellent complement to informative feedback and comes in many forms, including praise, salary increases, promotions, and special privileges.

Corrective feedback has a negative quality factor built in and is also an appropriate complement to informative feedback. Before giving corrective feedback,

- the employee must understand what you are saying;

- the employee must accept the information; and

- the employee must be able to do something about it.

When you do decide to use corrective feedback:

1. Get to the point

2. Allow a reaction

3.   Get agreement

4.   Develop a plan

5.   Summarize

6.   Follow-up

Handling Feedback

- Be selective

- Be specific

- Be prompt

- Be descriptive

- Be sensitive

- Explore alternatives

Supervisory No-Nos

1.   Treating individuals unequally because of sex, culture, age, academic or religious background, etc.

2.   Breaking an employee's trust

3.   Blowing hot and cold emotionally

4.   Failing to follow basic policies and procedures

5.   Losing your cool in front of others

6.   Engaging in a personal relationship with someone you supervise

7.   Being indecisive (unable to make decisions)

What Do You Know About Your Employees?

1. What are your employees' goals for the future within the organization?

2. How do your employees prefer to receive information (e.g., memos, formal meetings, phone call, informal meetings, e-mails, texting)?

3. What is your employees' preferred style of working?
    ____ Very organized and highly structured
    ____ Moderately organized and structured
    ____ Little organization or structure

4. Are your employees
    ____ More introverted (Reflect inwardly and prefer quiet time for thinking about things)
    OR
    ____ More extroverted (Reflect outwardly and prefer talking about things with others)?

5. What are your employees' three outstanding workplace strengths?

6. How do these strengths help you in getting the job done?

7. What are your employees' three greatest developmental needs? How are you working with them to address those needs?

8. What are your employees' greatest workplace stressors?

9. What do you know about your employees' families? Are they single, married, or do they have significant others? Any children? Any grandchildren? Mom and dad still living? Any pets?

10. What are your employees' favorite hobbies, sports, or outside interests?

You and Your Supervisor Suggestions

- Check out how your supervisor prioritizes tasks.
- Try to end all conversations with your supervisor on a positive note.
- Seek to understand your supervisor's perspective.
- Think of your supervisor as a key client/customer and your advocate.
- Show your supervisor that you deliver what you promise.
- Speak well of your supervisor as it reflects well on you.
- Remain professional, however friendly you are with your supervisor.
- Understand how your boss usually reacts to conflict and spot changes early.
- Keep your supervisor updated about your career goals.
- Change the way you interact with your supervisor according to his or her style.
- Ensure that you are given authority along with additional responsibility.
- Identify what information your supervisor needs to know and give frequent updates.
- Update your supervisor on your latest achievements and learning.
- Note your supervisor's body language as an indicator of any likely conflict.
- Measure your work both qualitatively and quantitatively.

The To-Do List

Success as a Supervisor

- Treat everyone with respect. Never forget to say "please" and "thank you."

- Listen.

- Reflect on your actions as if you were the one on the receiving end.

- Fight for your people the way you would like your boss to fight for you.

- When an employee has a complaint, handle it promptly.

- Keep employees fully informed as to what is going on.

- Be accessible.

- Keep your temper in check—control your feelings.

- Maintain your personal ethical standards.

- Don't let work overwhelm you.

- Don't neglect your career.

- Don't neglect your family and friends.

- Maintain a sense of humor.

- Be flexible.

- Maintain a professional presence.

- Use tact and diplomacy.

- Leverage diversity.

Reinforcement

You are only as good as the people who work for you. Make sure your employees regularly receive the reinforcement they need. Employees like to know how they are doing. Take a few minutes every now and then to let your people know you appreciate their dependability and the contributions they are making. Many capable employees leave (mentally and/or physically) because their superiors take them for granted.

Meetings

If you are responsible for holding a meeting:

- Prepare a written agenda:

    - Distribute two days before the meeting.

    - Identify the meeting's starting and ending times.

    - Keep the length of the meeting to 60 minutes or less.

    - If longer than 60 minutes, allow for breaks.

    - Stick to it during the meeting!

- Have the attendees confirm their attendance.

- Observe your audience for restlessness and pause for breaks when needed.

- Give positive and attentive facial expressions.

- Listen to your audience.

- Make sure handouts, PowerPoint slides, and so on are ready and organized before the meeting.

- If the meeting strays off topic, remind the attendees of the agenda and suggest that unrelated matters be addressed at another time.

- Be professional, polite, and poised.

- At the end of the meeting, review the action items captured.

- Keep eye contact 80–90% of the time.

- As the meeting leader, thank people for attending.

- Follow up on action items after the meeting.

The Power Perch and Other Seating Concerns

The Power Perch

- The head of the table is the "power perch."

- Other important positions include the seats immediately to the right or left of the power perch, and the seat opposite the power perch (unless it's too far away).

Rectangular Tables vs. Round Tables

- Sitting at the head of a rectangular table implies a position of power.

- If you want to avoid giving off the impression of power, sit at the side of a rectangular table, which will give off more of an impression that you're open to negotiations and interaction.

- Round tables are far better if you're looking to troubleshoot a problem or you want to encourage all attendees to have input as equals.

- The nature of a round table doesn't imply any form of leader or "head" in terms of its importance.

- If you're hosting a meeting and you have a deputy or special guest, he or she should be seated to your right.

When Expecting Conflict

If you are leading a meeting in which you expect there may be two or three people who are all opposed to something you need to discuss, a good way to defuse the situation is to seat them all on the same side of the table but a few spaces away from each other. This placement will prevent the dissenting members from making eye contact among themselves, which is often used to instigate a hostile debate instead of a fair discussion of a particular issue.

The Challenge

My Thoughts and Action Items

1. What specific new challenges (questions, concerns, issues) do you anticipate as a new supervisor?

2. What specific strategies will you use to manage these challenges before you?

3. Complete the following statements.

   I am known for . . .

         a.

         b.

         c.

         d.

   By this time next year, I plan also to be known for . . .

         a.

         b.

   New skills and knowledge I will learn in the next 90 days include . . .

         a.

         b.

Chapter 11
Making the Transition

"What we call the beginning is often the end. And to make an end is to make a beginning. The end is where we start from."

—T. S. Eliot, *Little Gidding*

If you have read this far into the book, it may now be time to take some definite steps. What transition do you need to make? While the old Nike commercials say "Just Do It," you may need to map out your transition. Why the term *transition* rather than *change*? Because transition is not the same as change.

Change vs. Transition

- Change is the way things will be different; transition is **how you get through** the three stages to make the change work.

- Transition is the inner process by which you come to terms with a change, as you let go of the way things used to be and reorient yourself to the way that things are now.

228

- Transition is an **ongoing internal process**. Change is made up of events and is visible and tangible, while transition takes place inside of people.

- Change is all about the outcome you are trying to achieve; transition is about how you'll get there and how you'll manage things while you are en route.

- Change can happen quickly and can be sped up. Transition is a natural process that may take weeks, months, or even years.

Transitions

In *Transitions: Making Sense of Life's Changes* by William Bridges, *transition* is defined as the three-stage natural process of starting with an ending, transitioning through a neutral zone, and starting a new beginning. Note that there is overlap. There is not a clear lineation from one stage to another.

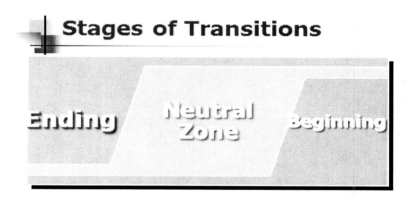

Stages of Transitions

Ending — Neutral Zone — Beginning

- Transition is the inner process through which people come to terms with a change as they let go of the way things used to be and reorient themselves to the way things are now.

- Managing transitions is the difficult process of letting go of an old situation, suffering the confusing nowhere of in-betweenness, and launching forth again in a new situation.

- We all have a lifetime of transitions.

Endings

Endings begin with letting go of. . . . ?

It means
- Making peace with the past
- Grieving a loss
- Feeling a range of emotions: anger, sadness, confusion, denial, fright, depression, relief, and joy

What do you want to let go of? Why?

I'm letting go of . . .	*I am letting go because . . .*

On Letting Go
or
Don't Drag a Dead Horse Across the Desert!

Don't let the past control your future. Remember this: "Don't drag a dead horse through the desert." The burden will kill you—your spirit. The dead horse represents past experiences, which may incorporate the demons that haunt you—your anger, your fears. The desert is part of your life journey. If you drag your fears, your anger, your negative past experiences through your life journey, it will destroy you.

Now, some people, when they realize they have a dead horse, will:

- blame society for the dead horse;

- form a committee to determine why the horse died;

- daily curse the dead horse;

- move the horse to another location in hopes the horse will revive itself;

- lie down and die next to the dead horse;

- get a stronger whip to beat the dead horse;

- sue the dead horse; or

- drag the dead horse, the dead weight, through the hot desert.

But my Native American friends taught me that you take what you can from the dead horse and move on. You take the hide of the horse to shield yourself from the heat of the sun during the day and keep you warm from the cold of the desert at night. You can take any sustenance (e.g., heart, liver) from the horse to help nurture you. In other words, you take the lessons (what can keep you moving forward) from the dead horse and move on. The horse is dead—the experience is dead—it no longer exists. Every ending is a new beginning.

Neutral Zone

What I will do to fulfill my potential?

It means

- Where the necessary reorientation and redefinition is taking place

- Often feeling worse (*Twilight Zone*)

- Resistance (the risk of launching a new beginning, doing and being what has never been done before)

> *"Every change looks like a failure in the middle."*
> —Rosebeth Moss Kanter, *The Change Masters*

Habits and Thoughts to Throw Away	New Ways of Behaving and Thinking

Beginnings

It means

- Developing new understandings
- Developing new attitudes (styles of thinking)
- Creating a new identity
- Making new commitments
- Carefully nurturing it all
- Feeling scared sometimes

Professional and Personal Transitions

Can you identify your dreams and aspirations for the next 2 years, 5 years, and 10 years?

	Professional	*Personal*
2 years		
5 years		
10 years		

Rewards and Benefits of Achieving Your Desires and Intentions	*Consequences of <u>Not</u> Achieving Your Desires and Intentions*

Identifying Past and Future Challenges

1. What are some challenges you have already faced in your career thus far? How did you deal with them?

2. What specific new challenges (questions, concerns, issues) do you anticipate in the next two years?

3. What specific strategies could you use to manage these challenges?

4. What resources are available to you to help achieve your desires, goals, and dreams?

5. Identify strategic steps that you can take in the next 12 months.

So Act Today!

What two things can you do to get the ball rolling in the direction you want? The actions don't need to be earth-shattering or dramatic; they just need to happen.

1.

2.

A Note on Writing Goals

This is a shortcut method that may aid you in writing your career goals. Please develop one goal—a specific goal that supports your professional growth and development—that you will strive to accomplish over the next 6–12 months. Remember: Your goal statement should capture what you really wish to achieve and use the SMART criteria.

S.M.A.R.T. Goal Writing

Specific	The goal should identify a specific action or eventthat will take place.
Measurable	The goal and its benefits should be quantifiable.
Achievable	The goal should be attainable, given the resources available to you.
Realistically high	The goal should require you to stretch some, but afford the likelihood of success.
Timely	The goal should state the time period in which it will be accomplished.

For example:

Specific: What is going to be done, when, and by whom?	I will read and then report on emotional intelligence. I will download the books on my computer or Kindle.
Measurable: How will you quantify the goal?	I will read three books in five months.
Achievable: Is it doable? Can you really do what you want, and at the measure you established?	Five months is definitely long enough to read three books.
Realistically high: Something relevant to your goal that stretches you	I've never even read one book on this subject, so three books is a substantial amount of research for me and should prepare me very well for a report.
Timely: What interim time frames? By what date?	I will read at least ten pages every day for five months.

Write your goal here: _____

_____

_____

_____

Using the SMART method, list two action steps you can take **in the next two to three months** to move forward.

1.

2.

Finally . . .

On a Personal Note

I would like to share some personal thoughts at the conclusion of this book. Truly, I wish someone had given me this information when I first started out in my career. To be honest, I never thought of myself as even having a career; I just worked. Later I would find out this was not the case. I had embarked upon a lifelong career—I just didn't know it! A lot happened along the way, through education, experiences, and many challenges. I have learned much about career development and what it can mean to people in the workforce (with or without experience). For this reason, I wrote this second book. As I hope has been made clear, **this is not a how-to book**; this is a book about information that may be useful in mapping out your career.

My personal learnings to share:

- **You must have a game plan!** Where are you going and how will you get there?

- **Identify your brand.** How do you want to be perceived?

- **Identify your values.** What is important to you?

- **Be willing to make mistakes and to learn from them.**

- **Networking is worth it.** Remember it is not who you know but who knows you and your capabilities!

- **People skills are important.** You may have the best technical skills, but you must also have the people skills to succeed.

- **Everyone doesn't have to like you, but they must respect you.**

You see, I know you can do it. Even the best of us need suggestions, no matter what career stage we are in.

Answer Keys and Scoring Guides

Preface

First, a Quiz: What Do You Think?

Quiz on page xv

Best answers for workplace savvy:

1. Agree
2. Disagree: Always provide an agenda.
3. Agree
4. Disagree: You need to break eye contact occasionally and you need to remember the key points of the speaker.
5. Agree
6. Agree
7. Agree
8. Agree
9. Disagree: Both behaviors are rude; offensive smells (such as nail polish fumes) and personal grooming in public are inconsiderate to bystanders.
10. Agree
11. Disagree: Let the person know you have to get back to your job; that is why you are here.
12. Agree
13. Disagree: Looks childish and unprofessional.
14. Disagree: Workplace socials are an extension of the work environment, where people have the opportunity to share information and network.
15. Agree
16. Disagree: Make everyone an ally.
17. Agree
18. Disagree: At the lowest level, you can practice ethical political savvy.
19. Disagree: Fear does not create positive collaboration.
20. Agree

21. Disagree: Not only is this not politically savvy, it is never acceptable.
22. Disagree: Business ethics applies to all employees.
23. Disagree: Asking employees for feedback helps you make better decisions.
24. Agree
25. Agree

Chapter 5

What Conflict Management Style Should You Use?
Exercise on page 72

1. **Avoiding**. You have already spent a lot of time and emotional energy competing against Stella, and you have won. She is being fired on Friday. You can certainly avoid the issue of Stella's lateness for three more days.

2. **Competing.** The president of the company has told you he wants a more diverse workforce. You have done your part, but your boss is getting in the way. First, go to your boss and argue your case—that the applicant is the best qualified for the job and that if he is not hired he will probably file a complaint with the EEOC, which the company will probably lose. If your boss is not convinced then tell him you are going to take this matter to the company president. This is an issue where you feel that your strong belief in equal opportunity will be seriously compromised if your boss's statement is allowed to go unchallenged. But be prepared with a plan B, an alternative course of action, in the unlikely event that the president backs your boss.

3. **Collaborating.** You have almost a year to collaborate with your close-knit staff in coming up with a win-win solution to this problem—one that makes everyone happy. Collaboration takes time, so be prepared to hold multiple sessions with the employees. If you are concerned with taking time from their regular work, have the sessions over lunch (and pay for the lunch if you can). If all of you can't reach a collaborative agreement, then you can try for a compromise. Either way, employees are more likely to support the final decision because they know their voices have been heard and their ideas have been considered.

4. **Accommodating.** The summer interns have spent a month on this project and have come up with a proposal they think could work. You have a team that is willing to pilot the proposal. Even if it fails, it will not cost much. It has been five years since the similar proposal